NEW DIRECTIONS FOR COMMUNITY COLLEGES

Arthur M. Cohen   Florence B. Brawer
EDITOR-IN-CHIEF   ASSOCIATE EDITOR

R. Dean Gerdeman
PUBLICATION COORDINATOR

Developing Successful Partnerships with Business and the Community

Mary S. Spangler
Los Angeles City College

EDITOR

Number 119, Fall 2002

JOSSEY-BASS
San Francisco

ERIC®

Clearinghouse for Community Colleges

378.103
D489

DEVELOPING SUCCESSFUL PARTNERSHIPS WITH BUSINESS AND THE COMMUNITY
Mary S. Spangler (ed.)
New Directions for Community Colleges, no. 119
Arthur M. Cohen, Editor-in-Chief
Florence B. Brawer, Associate Editor

New Directions for Community Colleges is indexed in Current Index to Journals in Education (ERIC).

Microfilm copies of issues and articles are available in 16mm and 35mm, as well as microfiche in 105mm, through University Microfilms Inc., 300 North Zeeb Road, Ann Arbor, Michigan 48106-1346.

ISSN 0194-3081   electronic ISSN 1536-0733   ISBN 0-7879-6329-1

NEW DIRECTIONS FOR COMMUNITY COLLEGES is part of The Jossey-Bass Higher and Adult Education Series and is published quarterly by Wiley Subscription Services, Inc., A Wiley Company, at Jossey-Bass, 989 Market Street, San Francisco, California 94103-1741, in association with the ERIC Clearinghouse for Community Colleges. Periodicals postage paid at San Francisco, California, and at additional mailing offices. POSTMASTER: Send address changes to New Directions for Community Colleges, Jossey-Bass, 989 Market Street, San Francisco, California 94103-1741.

SUBSCRIPTIONS cost $66.00 for individuals and $142.00 for institutions, agencies, and libraries. Prices subject to change.

THE MATERIAL in this publication is based on work sponsored wholly or in part by the Office of Educational Research and Improvement, U.S. Department of Education, under contract number ED-99-CO-0010. Its contents do not necessarily reflect the views of the Department or any other agency of the U.S. Government.

EDITORIAL CORRESPONDENCE should be sent to the Editor-in-Chief, Arthur M. Cohen, at the ERIC Clearinghouse for Community Colleges, University of California, 3051 Moore Hall, Box 951521, Los Angeles, California 90095-1521. All manuscripts receive anonymous reviews by external referees.

Cover photograph © Rene Sheret, After Image, Los Angeles, California, 1990.

Printed in the United States of America on acid-free recycled paper containing at least 20 percent postconsumer waste.

CONTENTS

ACKNOWLEDGMENTS

Mary Spangler would like to acknowledge the assistance of Fred Piegonski of Los Angeles City College in developing this volume. His work was crucial in supporting her effort to reach out to authors across the country—communicating with them regularly and coordinating their efforts, always with an eye on the calendar. During the past year, he has made numerous calls, written many letters, and personally kept the communication flowing between the editor and the staff at ERIC. His support was instrumental in ensuring a timely and well-developed publication. Also, the personal interest of Arthur Cohen, a long-time mentor to the editor, has been deeply appreciated.

EDITOR'S NOTES

Recent developments in community college programming include international education, electronic delivery systems, workforce education, and economic development. Success in these less traditional areas often involves collaborations and partnerships with other community colleges, business, industry, and the community in general. The position of community colleges in the middle of the educational hierarchy—between K–12 and the university—enables them to move easily and comfortably along that continuum as circumstances demand, as ideas arise, and as resources shrink and expand. These institutions are conditioned to be flexible and responsive. Happily, many of them also have people who possess the ingenuity to configure the resources in unexpected, creative, and groundbreaking ways.

This volume addresses the theme of collaboration and partnership between community colleges and business and the community by focusing on credit-based examples of some of the more innovative connections. The process behind the development of the model relationships should be useful to the practitioner wanting to develop or modify a similar program in a different setting. Each chapter describes the ingenuity of individuals committed to establishing a relationship based on a recognized need or opportunity. Each chapter offers insights into how the partnership connection was made; what time, energy, and resources were needed to develop the partnership; what challenges had to be overcome on the way to success; and what type of support is necessary for their continuation. Perhaps even more significant to the discussion, however, is a consideration of the wide-ranging benefits, both intended and unexpected, that result with successful partnerships.

The Statewide Advisory Committee for Work-Based Learning and Employment Services highlighted the importance and "good sense" of building powerful partnerships with business and the community in saying: "It enriches the quality of education by adding current and relevant information and an awareness of state-of-the-art technologies and trends. It creates work-based learning opportunities such as internships and job shadowing. It provides classroom speakers and attractive jobs for students. It makes available access to a variety of needed resources" (California Community Colleges Chancellor's Office, 2001, p. 2).

This volume does not discuss K–12 partnerships or relationships with four-year institutions in order to focus on ways in which community colleges can be and ultimately are connected with their local communities for the benefit of their students.

In Chapter One, David Buettner, Michael Morrison, and Marge Wasicek describe the "seeds" of successful partnerships, providing a conceptual framework for the remaining chapters. Key elements they identify include shared mission, consolidation of redundant activities, strategic growth, expanded economic opportunity, and access to and conservation of resources. They also address the challenges of preparation, leadership support, flexibility, and reduced autonomy. A case study shows how the concepts apply to their experiences at North Iowa Area Community College. The discussion of challenges is an important reminder of the need for a realistic consideration of the partnering strategy. Their experiences with successful partnerships in health care, workforce development, manufacturing, and entrepreneurship illustrate that these types of relationships, when founded on sound principles, can transform the nature of the community college while providing access to more opportunities than increased resources alone.

In Chapter Two, Lori Sundberg from Carl Sandburg College in Illinois examines the partnership connection from the perspective of the need to create value and benefit for all the partners, especially when private business is involved. The chapter describes the gradual process through which this college established a model partnership with Maytag Galesburg-Refrigeration and addressed the inevitable bureaucratic challenges, including responsiveness issues, governance, coordination, and cost sharing, that emerged from the partnership. There was unprecedented cooperation between the business community and the college because the industry partner recognized that the college could respond to its need for a skilled workforce. A key element in the creation of the Center for Manufacturing Excellence was the college's commitment to and involvement with the community.

Successful partnerships offer benefits on many levels. Art Tyler chronicles in Chapter Three how Los Angeles City College united with the community and captured national attention by transforming some valuable but underused property on a forty-eight-acre urban campus into a golf driving range. The chapter traces in detail how the environment enabled the partnership to flourish and the project to develop as it moved its way through a complex approval process. Although there were significant challenges, the benefits for the community outweighed them. This story illustrates how thinking creatively and being willing to chart new territory can offer many benefits.

In Chapter Four, John Allen presents in considerable detail the development of a unique partnership between Illinois Valley Community College and the International Brotherhood of Electrical Workers. In order to overcome a series of challenges, including developing the associate degree in applied sciences in electrical construction technology, working with sister colleges to get them to agree to collaborate, receiving approval from state and local boards, and drawing up a contractual agreement, the partners needed commitment, trust, cooperation, and vision. The curriculum, entrance requirements, and costs for the degree program are outlined. The chapter also identifies the benefits to the college and to the union and its members, especially the apprentices enrolled in the program.

In Chapter Five, Harvey S. Irlen and Frank Gulluni of Asnuntuck Community College in Connecticut describe how a partnership joining the college with the community, local chamber of commerce, and a number of private-sector manufacturers funded, marketed, and opened a manufacturing technology center to provide formal training that would benefit all the partners, both short-term and long-term. The authors recognize how critical it is in the workforce development arena for the customer and the student to be competently served. In addition to enumerating the contents of a unique four-level technology cluster, the authors identify the many positive outcomes of the partnership. Most notable is that the center has had documented success with its new program in upgrading the skills and abilities of the incumbent worker and eighteen- to twenty-two-year-olds in the field of metal machining technology.

In Chapter Six Lou Anne Bynum of Long Beach City College in California describes perhaps the most complex and ambitious example of a partnership in this volume. The size and time line of the grant that funded the collaborative alone would qualify it for the honor. However, the involvement of eight colleges, twenty-seven cities, industry, and public and private organizations significantly increased the level of coordination required for success. The discussion covers the partnership's operational structure and project components, participant characteristics, performance expectations for the consortium, and the series of challenges in administering a comprehensive college-and-industry-based training project in the Alameda Corridor. The purpose of the collaborative was to prepare local residents for jobs in the region's critical construction and trades industries. The project was successful in contributing to economic development and continuous workforce improvement in California.

Chapter Seven looks at student learning experiences that build community relationships. Linda Woiwod of Skagit Valley College in Washington State details a nationally recognized Learning Into Action program that ambitiously engages students in a full range of service learning activities that benefit the college, the community, and the students themselves. It is grounded in the belief that general education is more meaningful when students integrate acquired skills and knowledge into action. A unique feature of this program is the faculty's central role. The chapter covers the program's basic design elements and approach and looks at a broad range of existing partnerships and activities.

In Chapter Eight, Kathleen S. Hurley of Valencia Community College in Florida presents a partnership between an independent college program and a strong business advisory council that has guided and supported the Center for High-Tech Training for Individuals with Disabilities. Funded through state, federal, and private grants, the center—with a unique combination of design and concepts and a curriculum that supports the needs of the local business community—prepares individuals with severe physical disabilities for challenging high-tech careers. Although the chapter traces the center's formation, the discussion focuses on the critical role of the business advisory council, especially in the development of curriculum, and its active participation in the center's support functions. Also addressed are the challenges and benefits of maintaining such a partnership.

In Chapter Nine, the volume's guest editor, Mary S. Spangler, provides some observations on the common elements of success and the consistent challenges to overcome in creating and maintaining effective partnerships.

Finally, in Chapter Ten, with material drawn from the ERIC Clearinghouse for Community Colleges, Fred Piegonski of Los Angeles City College reviews a range of practitioner-oriented studies, models, and guides addressing partnerships between community colleges and community organizations. Purposely excluding educational intersegmental relationships, the review focuses on relationships with business and industry in the private sector. The readings are categorized into current community college partnerships, the development process leading to partnerships, statewide reports that include recommendations, handbooks with assessment materials, and one objective study measuring economic benefits. Additional sources for further reading conclude the chapter.

Mary S. Spangler
Editor

Reference

California Community Colleges Chancellor's Office Statewide Advisory Committee for Work-Based Learning and Employment Services. "Partnering with Employers. A Guide to Building Powerful Partnerships: Best Practices and Tips for Success." Sacramento: California Community Colleges Chancellor's Office, 2001.

MARY S. SPANGLER is president of Los Angeles City College, California.

1

A series of partnerships at North Iowa Area Community College have been founded on concepts critical to long-term success. The benefits extend beyond increased resources to make partnering an operational strategy.

Successful Experiences with Making Partnering an Operational Strategy

David L. Buettner, Michael C. Morrison, Margery Wasicek

Early in their existence, high-performing community colleges discovered the power of leveraging their resources through partnerships. These institutions quickly learned that when several entities choose to invest their collective resources to work toward a common end, the results usually outshine independent efforts. Today, many community colleges have elevated partnering to a key operational strategy. As they have done so, a body of knowledge about partnering has emerged.

The underlying concepts are basic and easy to understand. For our purposes, *partnering* is a formal collaboration. It is a mutually beneficial and well-defined relationship entered into by two or more organizations to achieve common goals. In the best such relationships there is a commitment to shared goal setting, a jointly developed structure, shared responsibility and accountability for success, and shared input of resources and distribution of rewards (Mattessich and Monsey, 1992).

This chapter begins with a discussion of the "seeds," or desired elements, of a partnership, and then follows with a case study of North Iowa Area Community College and its experiences with several partnerships. It concludes with a discussion of several common challenges that exist in partnership relationships. Recommended strategies and assessments that can be used in the development of new partnerships are offered.

Seeds of Partnership

This section describes elements or situations that can enhance the development and maintenance of a sound partnership.

NEW DIRECTIONS FOR COMMUNITY COLLEGES, no. 119, Fall 2002   © Wiley Periodicals, Inc.

Shared Mission and Goals. Every community is made up of various entities, each with its own mission and priorities. Although the diversity and scope of the missions represented in any community are substantial, so is the overlap between them. A typical community college strives to enrich the personal and professional opportunities of its learners and the economic development of its community through the educational programs and services it offers. In that community, there is, perhaps, a large regional medical center that also strives to enhance the quality of life of those same people but through healthy living and quality health services. Businesses operating there, in addition to their fundamental objective of making a return for their owners, may also declare an intent to enhance the quality of life of their customers and employees, if not the community as a whole. It is within these overlapping interests that the most promising seeds of successful partnerships are often found, for it appears that when a partnership emanates from an overlapping but noncompetitive mission, its potential and potential durability are greatest.

Common Activities. Sometimes when the ultimate missions seem unrelated, the means used to achieve those divergent missions can overlap. Overlapping means or activities, albeit for different ends, add substantially to the potential for partnering. For example, most community colleges see training as a reason for their existence, often making reference to it in mission or institutional purpose statements. A large regional medical facility engages in substantial training but for a more indirect reason. It strives to develop or maintain highly skilled workers in order to be able to provide high-quality health care. Although accrediting and licensing bodies and the realities of how quality health care is achieved may make training an everyday and fundamental aspect of operations, one would not necessarily expect to find references to education and training in a medical facility's mission and purpose statements. Yet education and training activities take considerable time, money, and effort that might otherwise be allocated to direct health care efforts.

Growing Strategically with Good Company. When mission and means do not directly lead to interest in partnering, some partnerships can promise political returns. Political leaders, often in regulatory or resource allocation roles, tend to see merit in the efficiencies of collaboration and sharing that most partnerships seem to offer. Elected leaders generally look favorably on entities that demonstrate efficient use of resources or more than good-faith interest in regulatory matters. Consumers may also grant benefits to partners as a result of their positive views of the association. Sometimes one partner's good reputation extends to its partnerships, and to some extent, therefore, to the other partners. Of course, the opposite may also be true. Choosing *a* partner or choosing *to* partner should always involve evaluation of the resulting partnership's effect on all partners' reputations and credibility.

Economic Opportunity. Some partnerships bring one or all partners expanded business opportunities. The rewards of association can go beyond the directly political to include economic opportunity and other returns expected from close relationships, a knowledge of good business opportunities, personal business connections, and especially participation and involvement in relevant activities. Being in the right place when a partnership opportunity presents itself comes from scanning the environment and knowing the resources available. Having relationships with the people who can assist in making connections with potential partners is critical in making the most of economic opportunities. These often come through connections with chambers of commerce or business bureaus. Involvement in community activities and a proximity to business connections help institutions know about and understand the problems or need for services. These connections often can produce opportunities where other forms of customer service—direct advertising of the college's services and resources—fall short.

In the end, successful partnerships must produce real gains in productivity and efficiency in order to thrive, if not survive. Usually, these gains come from resources the partners bring to the joint venture. When resources are pooled, the partnership can provide access to better or more resources than either entity is likely to have on its own, as the next section describes.

Leveraged Resources. The combined strength of partners may enable access to resources not otherwise available. Certainly, some funding agencies view partnerships or consortia in a positive light. And almost all funding sources view a strong suitor more positively than a weaker alternative. Sometimes the critical resources are not financial but rather talent, equipment, facilities, or even licenses. Often partnerships grow out of a pursuit of efficiency and economies of scale. Reduced overlap or duplication of effort and simple economies of scale can lower the investment required by either partner.

Each of these factors affects the viability and strength of a partnership. Shared or related mission elements, along with overlapping methods or activities (combined with good results, both political and real), make for the most durable and vigorous partnerships. Undertakings lacking one or more of these attributes can and do thrive, but they must do so without the natural valences these key elements provide.

A Case Study: North Iowa Area Community College

This section describes the experiences of one Iowa community college as it developed several partnerships and provides examples of how partnering as a strategy has redefined the nature of the college by giving it access to greater resources. The review is not intended as a detailed discussion of how or why the partnerships were formed. Instead, it focuses on the range of partnerships the college has been able to develop in order to illustrate why recognizing and acting on opportunities are critical to creating such connections.

At North Iowa Area Community College, partnering has become an integral element of institutional life. With ambitions and demands for services that extend well beyond its own resources, the college has used progressive partnerships as a means to greater mission fulfillment. Today, the college is involved in dozens of such partnerships. In addition to making available a greater number of services and opportunities, partnerships have also raised the quality level of many of those endeavors. Here are some noteworthy examples.

The Regional Health Education Center. Continuing education in the health care field, once a highly competitive and duplicated endeavor of the college and two competing hospitals, is now the mission of the Regional Health Education Center, a partnership between the college and Mercy Medical Center–North Iowa.

Now in its thirteenth year, with an annual budget approaching $1 million, the center generates a significant portion of the college's overall continuing education activity. In the first four or five years of its operation, annual expenditures were below levels of the independent entities before they joined together. Only later, when enrollment rose substantially above that of its inaugural year, did expenditures finally exceed the original levels of the partners. In addition to the obvious financial benefits, the partners gained by joining the college's expertise in community programming, training, and record-keeping systems with the industry's expertise in health care, people, facilities, and equipment.

The Workforce Development Center. With the demise of the Job Training Partnership Act (JTPA), which the college had administered in the region, it faced the loss of JTPA resources for its students and some of its programs. At the same time, the newly overhauled Iowa Job Service, now called the Iowa Workforce Development Department (IWD), struggled to transform its image in the eyes of the area's employers and residents who needed its services. The Workforce Development Center, a partnership of the IWD and the college, combines the college's closeness with employers, academic assessment expertise, and training capacity with the federal and state resources available for workforce development. The center serves as the placement agency for the college's graduates, leveraging the resources the college once allocated for this purpose. The college's economic development coordinator operates out of the center, lending the college's positive profile to the center's other interest, building more meaningful relationships with area employers.

The Business and Industry Partnership. Industrial continuing education can be done independently by a community college to some extent. But as the subject of that training becomes more and more integrated into the industry's product, service, or culture, a community college often cannot know enough about the internal details of the operation to succeed in making that industry understand the mutual benefits of partnering. What better way is there than to enlist the industry as a full partner in the planning, conceptualization, and delivery of training for its employees and managers? The Business and Industry Partnership uses this approach to gain a commitment from the businesses that the college partners with. And because many of the industries operating in the college's area are relatively small, gains have been made by enlarging the partnership processes to include collaborative training that crosses employers and settings. Cost efficiencies are at the center of this approach, but in reality, the very existence of much of the training is due to the partnership's ability to offer training that is inexpensive and highly tailored to industry needs.

Murphy Manufacturing Technology Center. When ambition or demand exceeds available resources, a partner with a similar interest in the goals can come to the rescue. Expanded training to support advanced manufacturing was in great need throughout the region. Local schools and the college shared an interest in responding, but neither had sufficient resources to address the opportunity. A partnership between the state economic development entity, the college, local schools, area employers, and a local industrialist made the state-of-the-art Murphy Manufacturing Technology Center possible. The college leads the effort, but each partner has a continuing interest in the operation of the center.

The Community Auditorium. The North Iowa Area Community College serves as the home for a twelve-hundred-seat performing arts facility that is heavily used by local schools, the college, and touring performers and presenters. No one agency in the region had the resources to construct and operate such a facility. By pooling responsibility and resources, the goal was achieved. The Community Auditorium's operation continues to be supported by community investments and users.

Buena Vista University–Mason City Center. "When is North Iowa Area Community College going to become a four-year college?" was for years a popular question directed to college officials. The reality is that Iowa has an oversupply of senior-college opportunities, but they are not well distributed. By partnering with Buena Vista University (BVU), North Iowa Area Community College was able to address local demands for upper-division opportunities without taking on the financial or political burden that would have accompanied any attempt to broaden its own mission. Today the BVU center is a rent-paying partner, extending the usefulness of college facilities, equipment, and personnel.

Pappajohn Entrepreneurial Center. The college aspired to boost entrepreneurship in the region as an economic development strategy but lacked the resources to staff and support such an effort. Thanks to a partnership between a successful venture capitalist alumnus and the college, a highly visible effort was launched. Today, the Pappajohn Entrepreneurial Center is a partnership between the college, the University of Iowa, the

Kauffman Foundation, and other Iowa community colleges. To date, it has offered training to sixteen hundred aspiring entrepreneurs who have started over 225 new businesses.

Common Challenges

This section describes the attributes and qualities necessary to maintain healthy relationships.

Good Preparation. Successful partnering requires supportive behaviors by all partner organizations that go beyond the obvious. Early in the life of a successful partnership, cultures may clash, fuzzy expectations become clearer, and initial viewpoints may be tested. Mundane or routine processes and procedures must sometimes be decided on or developed. And when a partnership includes employees with loyalties to one or the other partners, adopting one partner's practices and procedures can be both helpful and challenging.

The prudent leader will recognize that traditional cultures, reward structures, and decision-making practices that foster increased levels of specialization and fragmentation inhibit change in many organizations. Strategies need to be developed in the preparation stage to overcome or limit such barriers to effective partnerships. Most importantly, leaders need to address the human dimension of change. To be successful, strategic partnerships must go beyond the mechanics of the operation and address the human issues of building community, commitment, and trust.

Commitment and Importance of CEOs. It is absolutely essential that the CEOs of the partnering organizations clearly define the purposes of the partnership and how the partners will measure and define success. A united executive front with a comprehensive vision of the future is a necessary but insufficient condition for success. Through their actions, the CEOs must model the change process inherent in organizational alignment. They must form a strategic alliance to map and guide the change process. They must help others in their respective organizations to redefine roles and relationships and build a consensus around the vision for the future. They must foster commitment and coordination for successful partnerships. CEOs must examine and realign resources and systems with new directions. Successful delegation of responsibility and empowerment of staff to achieve agreed-upon goals are essential. CEOs also have crucial responsibilities for identifying and monitoring measures of effectiveness. Prudent interventions will be called for when outcomes fail to meet desired ends. Celebrating success will also provide the incentive for future goal achievement. Without leadership and commitment from the top, a partnership has a dim future.

Flexibility. At times a partner may need or want something from the partnership that is not important or even meaningful to the other partners. The strongest partnerships are those in which such needs or wants are carefully evaluated and handled by all concerned. One partner's insensitive requests can test the patience and flexibility of the others. Narrow self-interest can result in behavior that may be viewed as exploitative by others.

A narrow perspective by any partner can lead to less willingness to accommodate the specific needs or wants of other partners. With little room for flexibility or accommodation for activities that are particularly important and meaningful to only one or a few partners, a partnership may weaken its overall value to its members.

The strongest partnerships are those in which there is considerable perceived benefit by each of the partners. Each partner perceives the greatest value to the extent that its special needs and wants can be accommodated.

Less Autonomy. The price of successful partnering may be a significant loss of autonomy. Partners that enter collaborations without adequate understanding of the need for or commitment to shared decision making will surely suffer. As partnering becomes systemic in an organization, managing or guiding that organization takes on new complexity.

Conclusion

Senior-level leaders who desire to build new systems through partnerships must develop new roles, relationships, skill sets, and operating methods so they can become more adaptive and responsive to changing partnership realities. Systems thinking and systems building are among the most important skill sets, promising to elevate partnerships to higher levels of performance and customer satisfaction. Learning organizations, acting and thinking systemically, make deliberate and prudent decisions to reduce organizational autonomy with expectations that customers will be better served through the partnership. Leaders will be challenged in this environment to develop their skills to continually clarify and deepen their personal visions for the future. They must learn how to see the current reality more clearly. The partnership reality will surely be more complex, requiring leaders to see interrelationships and patterns that escape the vision of others (Senge, 1990). Having seen interlocking patterns and opportunities, the servant-leader (Greenleaf, 1977) will, through the development and implementation of an effective partnership, reduce his or her own power and institutional autonomy for the fulfillment of higher values and goals.

References

Greenleaf, R. K. *Servant Leadership: A Journey into the Nature of Legitimate Power and Greatness.* New York: Paulist Press, 1977.

Mattessich, P. W., and Monsey, B. R. *Collaboration: What Makes It Work.* St. Paul, Minn.: Amherst H. Wilder Foundation, 1992.

Senge, P. *The Fifth Discipline: The Art and Practice of the Learning Organization.* New York: Doubleday, 1990.

DAVID L. BUETTNER, *currently president of Fox Valley Technical College, Wisconsin, was previously president of North Iowa Area Community College, Iowa.*

MICHAEL C. MORRISON *is vice president of academic affairs at North Iowa Area Community College, Iowa.*

MARGERY WASICEK *is executive director of the Regional Health Education Center, a partnership of North Iowa Area Community College and Mercy Medical Center–North Iowa.*

2

The Center for Manufacturing Excellence, which houses a business incubator and provides many creative ideas for workforce development programs, has made a significant impact on its community.

Building Partnerships with Business That Make a Difference

Lori L. Sundberg

Doing more with less has increasingly been the challenge for community colleges over the last ten years (Burd, 2001; Schmidt, 2000). Carl Sandburg College is no exception. In fact, it has had to develop unique and creative solutions to achieve the 10 percent increase in credit hours and the 40 percent increase in enrollment that has occurred over the same time period (Illinois Community College Board, 1990–2000). In the school's rural, west central Illinois district, where economic hardship and declining assessed valuations have become commonplace, developing partnerships with other entities in the community is a logical solution to the problems of diminishing resources and lagging enrollments (Northrup, 1994). The bigger question for representatives of Carl Sandburg College has been how to develop and structure these partnerships so that the pooling of resources benefits all.

Partnerships are emerging between public school systems and colleges, four-year universities and community colleges, and to a lesser degree between colleges and businesses (Murtadha-Watts, Belcher, Iverson, and Medina, 1999; Brouillette, 2001; Lozada, 1996). Because profit is essential for businesses to operate and remain viable, the benefit becomes an even more important component in partnerships with them. Maintaining the partnership can best be achieved by continually assessing the value being delivered and by being flexible and responsive to the fast-changing needs of business.

This chapter outlines the process that Carl Sandburg College used in developing successful partnerships in the community, and particularly its partnership with Maytag Galesburg-Refrigeration. Through these partnerships the college was able to build the Center for Manufacturing Excellence,

New Directions for Community Colleges, no. 119, Fall 2002 © Wiley Periodicals, Inc. 13

a thirty-thousand-square-foot manufacturing facility both for college industrial programs and for customized and contract training for area manufacturers. Any new and innovative endeavor presents challenges and these are
also discussed, along with the current status of the college's partnerships.

The Partnership Development Process

Representatives from Carl Sandburg College found that the process and the
critical elements of developing partnerships with either businesses or other
educational institutions were simple in theory but complex in practice. The
process began with the community involvement of college representatives.
It is impossible to form partnerships without both the committed support
of the institution's top leadership and its representatives' involvement with
the community. College Sandburg College administrators and faculty recognize the need to participate actively on community boards of directors
and in service clubs and professional organizations. The president is actively
involved in the Galesburg Area Chamber of Commerce, the Galesburg
Regional Economic Development Association, and various other civic organizations. In addition, the president has hosted many town meetings
throughout the college district—three thousand square miles—in which he
and other college representatives meet with businesspeople and residents
to listen to and learn about the issues that are of concern to that particular
community. He and the board of trustees firmly believe in the idea "of putting the 'community' back into the mission of this community college"
(Donald G. Crist, personal communication, May 14, 2001). Thus, college
representatives and leaders try to understand and assess the concerns and
needs of the community as much as economic development leaders
and local businesses do. Because the administrative team serves on various
community boards, issues of concern or interest are brought back to the college and discussed in administrative staff meetings. If further input and
analysis are needed, college leaders get back in touch with the organization
or the people in the community who raised the concerns or ideas to discuss
them further. The college president and the cabinet, with guidance from the
board of trustees, then decide which issues need further investigation. With
this continued involvement, local business leaders have come to recognize
and respect the role that Carl Sandburg College plays in the community.

From this kind of connection, a natural exchange of needs and ideas
starts flowing. For example, through discussions with the superintendent
of the local school district, the president of Knox College (a private liberal
arts institution), and the executive director of the Galesburg Area Chamber
of Commerce, it became clear that the region was lacking in technology
resources. The idea of a state-of-the-art educational technology center complete with facilities for distance learning, satellite conferencing, and public
computer labs designed to serve all three institutions, area businesses, and
the general public grew from those discussions and became a reality in

1996. This partnership captured the attention of many people, particularly state and federal legislators and representatives from the U.S. Department of Education, as a unique and innovative way to pool resources to achieve a greater good. Today, the facility is owned and operated by all three entities. It was largely funded by local businesses that could see the value in using the center for their own technology training needs.

The Center for Manufacturing Excellence (CME)

Due in part to the success of the educational technology center and the recognition it achieved from being involved in the project, Carl Sandburg College gained the credibility it needed to move forward and develop partnerships for other much-needed projects in the community. It was the gradual process of building relationships, working together with other organizations in the community, and gaining trust as a reliable partner that led the college to another project: the Center for Manufacturing Excellence. Over time, these relationships further evolved into a key partnership with Maytag Galesburg-Refrigeration, a major manufacturer in the area.

Carl Sandburg College is located in a rural district, largely a manufacturing and farming community. In 1996, several manufacturers approached the college to discuss their need for a training facility that would address the severe workforce shortage they were currently experiencing. Furthermore, they anticipated additional shortages in the next five to ten years as a result of retirements. Nationwide, it is projected that in the next ten years over one-third of the current manufacturing workforce will retire. West central Illinois manufacturers were realizing that they were in the same situation. Finally, many current employees needed retraining for the higher-tech jobs emerging in many manufacturing facilities.

Maytag Galesburg-Refrigeration, located in Galesburg, Illinois, is the largest manufacturer in the district, with about twenty-four hundred employees. Maytag, like other manufacturers, was struggling to acquire and maintain a workforce skilled enough to work with the more technologically sophisticated equipment used in factories today. The manufacturers increasingly needed workers who were proficient in math, computer technology, and quality measures. The average high school graduate was no longer skilled enough for many of these firms. In early discussions with manufacturers, the college was the first to admit that, although it already had industrial programs and certificates in place, these programs were not sufficient and did not address the emerging need for a technologically trained workforce. Manufacturers had new problems that needed to be addressed with fresh ideas. In the end, area manufacturers and the college formed a partnership to develop an industrial training facility that would be state-of-the-art.

Owners and representatives of manufacturing firms, leaders from the chamber of commerce and economic development council, and college leaders traveled to several industrial training centers across the country to do research for this project. They visited several outstanding facilities but found that the training centers were operated either by community colleges or by independents. None was run as a partnership between private industry and a community college. The CEO of Midstate Manufacturing commented later at a fundraising event, "We noticed a lack of cooperation in those cities" ("Maytag Shows the Money," 1997, p. A1). The people involved in this initial research-gathering assignment felt that any industrial training facility they developed would be better served by a partnership between the college and private industry. Each side had its own expertise and insights that would be enhanced by the other. How to achieve that structure or balance was unknown at the time, but clearly there was not going to be an existing model to emulate. Although the leaders of this project knew that they were embarking on new territory, they were supported by a virtually unprecedented level of cooperation between the business community and the college.

After eighteen months of research and planning, the concept of the Center for Manufacturing Excellence was conceived. At a cost of $2 million, the facility was planned to house state-of-the-art manufacturing equipment and provide customized training for manufacturers as well as the college's degree and certificate programs. The facility was planned as a partnership between the college, the manufacturing community, and the educational technology center that had already been built. Although the CME was built on the college campus, today it is governed by its own board of directors, which includes the college president, two college trustees, three manufacturers, a member of the business and technology center, the executive director of the chamber of commerce, the director of the Galesburg Regional Economic Development Association, and a superintendent of a local public school system. The CME hires and employs its own staff. The strength of this facility is its flexibility to respond to local manufacturing needs as they arise because the college's typical constraints of operating in district boundaries or offering fixed-schedule classes are not present.

Maytag Galesburg-Refrigeration is an important partner in the facility and in fact was instrumental not only in its conception but also in its development and funding. As stated earlier, the project directly responded to the company's needs for a workforce current in skills, abilities, and knowledge, as required by an increasingly competitive economy. Maytag committed personnel to the planning of the venture and was the first manufacturer to come forward to kick off the fundraising campaign with the largest private-sector gift that the campaign would ultimately receive. Maytag in many ways led the fundraising charge and set the standard for other contributors. Its contribution of $250,000 toward the total goal of $2 million illustrated the importance it placed on the facility. Maytag believed so strongly in this project that the CEO of the corporation was the guest of honor and speaker at the fundraising kickoff. The Center for Manufacturing Excellence was a project that promised to provide significant training possibilities for its workforce, and the company hoped this training would transfer into a competitive advantage in the marketplace. The CEO that evening summarized the entire eighteen-month planning period that had preceded the fundraising effort when he made the following statement: "We can't afford turf in today's world. . . . because your competition can come from anywhere in the world. The winner is the one that's going to be the best." A spokesperson for the Carl Sandburg College trustees echoed those thoughts on behalf of the board in saying, "Everyone wins here. We're on the leading edge" ("Maytag Shows the Money," 1997, p. A1).

Challenges Addressed by CME Partners. As with any new endeavor, there were significant challenges. In addition, whenever an endeavor is completely new, there is a learning curve on all sides, and the more innovative the project the greater the learning curve will be. First and foremost, representatives from the college, Maytag, and the other manufacturers involved in the project were committed to listening to and trying to understand one another's positions and needs.

The most difficult issue they needed to face early on was how to deal with the process or bureaucracy of community colleges. Businesses have difficulty working in an educational bureaucracy and thus try to avoid it when possible. Yet in a community college, the bureaucratic process is central, and a partnership between both parties must navigate this organizational reality in order for there to be a successful outcome. Issues such as approvals by the state governing board—in this particular case, the Illinois Community College Board—and statutory regulations that must be adhered to, such as the use of architects, were contentious in early discussions. Businesses are accustomed to making decisions and acting on them—now. Whereas a for-profit business's prime audience is its stakeholders, the community college has multiple constituencies, both internal and external. The main way that this concern was dealt with was by both sides staying in constant dialogue. Fortunately, the project remained the focal point, and issues were resolved for the good of the project by compromising to meet the overall goal.

The second issue of concern was control or governance of the facility. Business leaders wanted to share control of hiring, scheduling, and oversight. They wanted the facility to be flexible and responsive to area manufacturers, and they wanted the facility to be known as a national training site. Although the college representatives understood why businesses wanted this control, the concept violated many of the college's current policies and procedures, such as for hiring, salary, and tenure. Once again, the two sides were able to work these issues through and find a mutually satisfactory solution for the board of directors with representation from the college, the manufacturing community, the chamber of commerce, and a public school system. The final resolution was that the director of the facility was hired by and reports solely to the CME board of directors. This position is not a college-funded position, so issues such as tenure and work schedule are not subject to the same rules as in the college. With the board of directors that was established to oversee the CME, every stakeholder has a vote, so neither the college nor the business leaders have more control or more influence than the other.

Although the CME is located on the college's main campus, it is a separate entity from the college. It has its own board of directors and hires its own personnel who do not work for the college. The college provides services to the CME, including general maintenance, security, and snow removal, but the CME was built with both private and public funding, so it is not solely a state-funded or state-owned project. Manufacturers provided the bulk of the costs and contributed approximately $1.4 million, with local legislators appropriating an additional $650,000 in Illinois state dollars. Manufacturers continue to use the facility for training; therefore, they are generating many of the dollars that pay the operating expenses.

Is this arrangement complicated? Yes. Does it cause a multitude of problems sometimes? Yes. For example, boundary issues are a primary concern because, in Illinois, community colleges have districts. Usually, a community college does not recruit students or even offer programs in a neighboring community college district, but the CME is different. Because the college is only a partner in the facility, it is not as constrained by those boundaries as the college would be if it were the sole deliverer. The college does make certain that none of its programs is advertised in neighboring districts, but if a CME program is available to its neighbors, it can be marketed in other districts. The college remains in contact with all of its neighboring colleges to ensure good communication and to make certain they are aware of what the CME is offering and what the college is offering.

Is this arrangement worth the outcomes? The answer is an overwhelming yes! The CME is now entering its second full year of operation, and more than 700 people have already taken advantage of training, with 230 of that total coming from Maytag alone. However, there are still issues. For example, how will the Center for Agriculture, Business, and Industry (CABI), which is part of the college, work in selling customized training with the director of the CME? In addition, the questions of which entity gets credit and how the reimbursement from the state should be shared are areas that were not considered in the planning stages but are now being reviewed. The college president states, "The key ingredient to the success of this partnership is trust. Throughout this project, everyone knew and trusted that people cared first and foremost for the project and any mistakes or misunderstandings were quickly resolved and put aside" (Donald G. Crist, personal communication, May 14, 2001). This attitude allowed everyone to focus on the project and not on positions.

Conclusion

The partnership with Maytag continues to progress. Currently, a new training program designed specifically for Maytag is doing well. Maytag has since worked with staff at the CME to develop a Maytag service repair training program that provides training for the entire region. Recently, the program was held at the CME, and Maytag had employees attend from all over the United States, Canada, and the Philippines. The company currently uses the CME an average of three times a month for various employee training activities.

Although the facility is still very new, all stakeholders, including Maytag, agree that it is moving in the direction of solving a very real workforce problem. It is not generating quite as much revenue as initially expected, but is covering its costs and the potential for growth is enormous as the economy begins to strengthen.

It is true that a partnership between a community college and business can accomplish more benefits with fewer resources, but doing the early, preliminary legwork in the community is essential. Without the CME, businesses would still be sending their employees elsewhere for training and incurring greater travel costs. With this local facility, more training can be provided and at a better price. Creating a climate that encourages dialogue from all sides sets the stage for ideas and creativity to flow. Partnerships should not be created as an easy solution to an old problem; rather, they should be created to address new, emerging issues. It is critical for businesses and community colleges to look for ways to create value and solve problems by working together.

Times have changed. Technology for many businesses is at the forefront, and new approaches are imperative if American businesses and institutions of higher education are going to remain competitive. The Maytag–Carl Sandburg College partnership is an example of a successful and innovative approach that solved a regional problem and is applicable in other areas. In fact, this concept is already being applied in neighboring areas. The first step is to sit down with local businesses to find out their needs and create a project that meets those needs. Funding is usually expected to be the most difficult issue, but in reality the most difficult part is making certain that the project does what it needs to do for the community. If that goal can be achieved, then local businesses will see the value and make the appropriate contributions.

References

Brouillette, L. "How Colleges Can Work with Schools." *Chronicle of Higher Education,* Feb. 23, 2001, p. B16.

Burd, S. "President Bush's Budget Plan Deals Multiple Blows to Community Colleges." *Chronicle of Higher Education,* Apr. 20, 2001, p. A34.

Illinois Community College Board. *Student Enrollments and Completions in Illinois Community College System.* Springfield: Illinois Community College Board, 1990–2000.

Lozada, M. "The Partnership Club." *Vocational Education Journal,* 1996, 71, 40–41.

"Maytag Shows the Money." *Galesburg Register-Mail,* Aug. 15, 1997, p. A1.

Murtadha-Watts, K., Belcher, A., Iverson, E., and Medina, M. "City Schools–City University: A Partnership to Enhance Professional Preparation." *NASSP Bulletin,* 1999, 83, 64–70.

Northrup, K. "Equalized Assessed Valuation for Illinois Community College Districts, 1883–1993." Parkland College, 1994.

Schmidt, P. "State Higher-Education Funds Rise Overall, But Growth Slows in Much of Nation." *Chronicle of Higher Education,* Dec. 15, 2000, p. A34.

LORI L. SUNDBERG *is director of institutional research at Carl Sandburg College, Illinois.*

Building a golf driving range on an urban community
college campus provides an example of entrepreneurial
partnering with a private developer. This project
reconnected the campus and community cultures and
helped reenergize the faculty and staff.

Developing Successful Community Partnerships: "Teeing Up" for Change

Arthur Q. Tyler

Every economic enterprise and business deal involves different circumstances, different advantages, and unique challenges. In the realm of enterprises engaged in by public agencies, partnerships with private entities are the most complex and often the most difficult to effect. However, they can also be the most rewarding and make the most efficient use of a public agency's resources. This chapter explores how a community college not only developed an underused piece of real estate but also created the impetus for changing the institution overall. The objective of the chapter is to provide a detailed illustration of what can be done if an institution remains flexible, has just a little vision, and perseveres.

This chapter begins by identifying the environment that enabled the partnership to take hold and then outlines how it was conceived and describes each partner's requirements for the project to be successful. It recounts some of the challenges that had to be overcome, the complex approval process involved, and the benefits of the project for the college.

The Need for a New View

In 1997, Los Angeles City College was a college in decline. Its infrastructure was perilously decayed, and its financial future looked bleak. Gangs had started to invade its sacrosanct quad and undermine the security needed in order for an intellectual environment to flourish. The faculty, staff, and administration struggled to overcome a projected $6.5 million deficit and all the implications associated with that condition in the wake of prior mismanagement, underfunding, and a 12 percent retroactive pay increase for faculty and staff.

NEW DIRECTIONS FOR COMMUNITY COLLEGES, no. 119, Fall 2002   © Wiley Periodicals, Inc.

In March 1997 the college hired a new president, and in June a new vice president of administration. The new leadership struggled to find ways to return the college to its earlier stature as a leader in the community and in the domain of education at large. At the same time, there was a need to find new ways of funding programs to help cushion the college from the ebb and flow of unpredictable state budget allocations. And the faculty and staff needed to regain a feeling of safety to allow a resurgence of unity and trust.

The first resolve of the college leadership was to clean up the campus and re-create a sense of well-being for all in the total college community. One of the biggest eyesores was a four-and-a-half acre parcel on the south end of the campus that faced a major traffic corridor. This area had once been home to a softball field and a field for such bygone athletics as archery. Now it was nothing more than a dumping ground for the community's and the college's discarded furniture and equipment.

This site was one of the main points of entry onto the campus because both freeway access points are nearby. Thus, the "front yard" of the college said clearly that no one cared about this place. It contributed to the sullen attitude that was pervasive among the college staff and faculty and to the feeling among gangs that this "turf" was theirs. The only questions to be resolved were these: What do we use it for? And how do we pay for it? The need for a creative use was apparent, but another challenge was to determine how to maintain the property for future growth while developing something new and wonderful.

Partnership Development and Processes

The partnership that Los Angeles City College and a private developer formed to build a golf driving range on the campus is an example of a successful community college partnership with the community. The concept was to build a new three-acre golf driving complex, complete with a putting green, pro shop, and restaurant. This enterprise would produce a guaranteed income, subsidized parking, and maintenance for the college while also providing a very profitable business for the developer. Although the project began with a chance meeting rather than through a formal process, the circumstances and timing were such that the partnership was able to move from concept to reality. The process that evolved became the model for the Los Angeles Community College District's later developmental programs at its other eight colleges. But, initially, as often happens, this "marriage" was more accidental than planned as two different entities found a common space in need of development.

The college is located close to Hollywood, where the old adage is, "Timing is everything in show business." Luckily for the college, the time had come for an opportunity for a partnership. The inspiration was Tiger Woods, whose phenomenal success has motivated millions, including inner-city minorities, to want to hit a little dimpled ball. Golf was on the minds of many in the late 1990s, including the developer, a successful Korean-American businessman who owns a real estate development firm near the college. He wanted to give members of his community, many of whom love the sport of golf, an opportunity to practice near their homes and workplaces in the Koreatown section of Los Angeles. The two urban practice facilities available there were small, and although somewhat successful, did not really give the customers what they needed. Golfers prefer to practice their skills on a full-length range, which should be at least two hundred yards long. The old facilities were both less than one hundred and fifty yards long; this meant that golfers could not use any of their long irons or woods effectively.

Many golf enthusiasts had to drive ten or twenty miles to a more suburban environment to practice, sometimes at a cost of one or two hours in travel time because of the traffic. In search of opportunities, the developer noticed that Los Angeles City College was the largest landowner in the area. He conceived a plan that he thought would help the college while simultaneously allowing him to bring his project to fruition. He was aware the college had a parking problem and realized that if the college built an adjacent parking structure, he could put his golf driving range on top of it. Assuming that the college would need help in funding the structure, he proposed to provide partial funding for the construction and a ground lease to help cover the remaining costs. After surveying the neighborhood, he took the initiative of calling for an appointment to explore the possibilities, and his request for a meeting was accepted.

The college leadership created the process for development of the project in conjunction with the private developer. All aspects of the concept were created anew because there had never been a similar development in the district. In addition, because the project was not incorporated into or conceived as part of a master planning process, the issues of feasibility and college support had to be thoroughly discussed and evaluated by the college at large. Throughout the process it was critical to keep the campus community informed of the progress.

The development steps were as follows:

Create a concept plan for the project.
Present the plan to the college's shared governance community.
Present the concept to local city officials and gain their support.
Conduct community-at-large forums to discuss the project and gather input and comments.
Incorporate the ideas into the project where feasible.
Present the plan to the community college district senior staff.
Gather support from the board of trustees.
Present the revised plan to the Los Angeles Planning Commission for approval of variances.

Upon city approval, present to the board of trustees for final approval of the plan and the mitigation of Environmental Impact Report and CEQA (California Environmental Quality Act) report.
Secure approval of architectural plans by Department of State Architecture.
Select the project management team and start construction.

Requirements of the Partners

Each partner had several important objectives that had to be addressed individually. The college leadership team, working with the developer, determined that the project would only be viable if the following objectives could be met:

- The project would not cost the college any money. The developer agreed to lease the property and build the project without any assistance from the college.
- The partnership would have to produce revenue for the college. The revenue would come from several sources, including rent, maintenance fees, and subsidized parking development. The new athletic and enhanced academic programs that would be offered added to the incentive, especially because the developer agreed to sponsor the athletic teams and the new academic program would generate additional funding. The college would add two golf teams before opening the golf range and subsequently double the number of golf classes.
- The facility had to be available some of the time for classes. The college would generate enrollment revenues by using the facilities for at least four hours four days per week.
- The facility had to aid in the overall cleanup of the area. The new building would also house a new police facility to provide community-based policing and a twenty-four-hour drop-in police community center. This development would also create a new impetus for remodeling the area and improving security on the south end of the college.
- The project had to help solve the parking problem by adding four hundred parking spaces for the college to use at no cost.
- The finished project had to help create a safe environment for learning. The improved security and well-lit facilities would enhance the area and create a sense of safety.

Similarly, the developer had objectives he needed to meet with the venture:

- The enterprise had to be profitable. The pro forma evaluation of profits from the project indicated that the developer would break even in less time than with most business ventures.
- The project had to be affordable. The college made the lease affordable during the development phase of the project.

- The operation had to have the image of "the best golf facility inside the city."

Over the next twelve months, the new partners established a relationship and mutual trust and developed a concept that would integrate the objectives and goals of both. This frankness was the key that ensured the partnership's survival through the challenges over the lengthy time from concept to completion. The college had also wanted to enhance its police facilities and determined that locating the police on a main thoroughfare would have a dramatic effect and reassure all who entered from the south and the freeways that this campus was a haven; it would be a visible sign that the college was, in fact, one of the safest places in Los Angeles.

The Challenges of the Partnership

Lewis Mumford (1952), a famous architectural and urban planning critic, once wrote in reference to the development of a modern city that "the embodiment of the modern city is in fact impossible until. . . . the cultural and educational purposes of the city have been outlined and until all of man's activities have been integrated into a balanced whole" (p. 2). The plan developed by the new partnership created the symbiotic relationship Mumford suggested. But was it balanced? Only the test of time and voices from the two interlocked communities—the city and the college—would confirm whether the balance could be achieved.

The idea, though creative, raised several new problems for the college and the residents of the community surrounding the off-campus parking structure. First, local residents and businesses were concerned that the new facility would create additional traffic and parking problems on already congested and narrow side streets. Second, residents were concerned about the height of the structure in an area where none of the other buildings was more than four stories high. Finally, one the most important challenges was how to integrate this project with the college mission.

To address the traffic issue, the developer conducted a traffic survey and proved that there would be no significant increase from his golf customers because only sixty-six patrons could be accommodated at one time. Furthermore, the college and developer emphasized that the additional parking for the students, created at no cost to the college, would reduce student parking in the residential areas nearby. Also, the developer and college agreed to work with several of the businesses and community resources, including two churches, that needed additional parking on the weekends by allowing them to use the new parking spaces.

As for the height of the structure, it was slated to exceed one hundred and fifty feet, meaning it would be more than one hundred feet taller than any other structure in the area. Residents were especially concerned about the light that might be generated from the lights on this structure. The developer hired a special lighting engineer who solved the problem by designing lights that did not emit light outside the range. This was demonstrated to the L.A. city planning administrator and the residents at a community hearing. The planning administrator lauded the effort, and the community's fears were put to rest.

One of the most difficult dilemmas for the college was to determine a fit with its mission and goals. The college, fortunately, had been conducting four golf classes as part of its physical education program. More significant was the fact that these classes were full despite the lack of adequate teaching facilities. The new facilities would allow the college to increase its offerings to ten classes per semester without any further curriculum development. Also, the athletic department could develop men's and women's golf teams. The developer agreed to be the sponsor of the two teams to increase further the benefit to the college.

The Approval Process

To make this project a reality a series of complex interactions among multiple bureaucracies had to be navigated. Once a model and architectural rendering were developed, the long process began of convincing the faculty and staff, the community, and two bureaucracies—the City of Los Angeles and the Los Angeles Community College District—that this project was a good idea and feasible. The partners developed a simple marketing approach to respond to the first two campus constituencies. Several open forums were held with the faculty and staff to explain the idea and concept. The initial time line was presented at four forums for the college population, including the students. The feedback from the forums was incorporated into the further development of the project.

Next, the college used the office of the local councilperson to organize the community forums. These were held both on and off the campus to encourage as much participation as possible. This inclusive approach was crucial to the success of the Los Angeles City Office of Planning hearing that followed. The critical issues of lighting, pollution, and traffic were easily resolved because the public supported the goals of the project, and they had been informed ahead of time.

The next step was to convince the community college district's board of trustees that the project had merit, was legal, and would be beneficial to the college. The board was concerned about whether the proposed use of the land would tie up the property for too long. It was also concerned about whether the developer was earnest in his intentions. These concerns were assuaged when an outside consultant was hired to verify the analysis of the benefits of the project. The consultant's conclusion was that it was not only a sound investment of space but also would provide the answers the college was looking for to help fix its parking dilemma. Furthermore, it made good business sense and offered an excellent return on the investment for the developer.

The developer put up "good faith" money that allowed the college to start cleaning up the site and other parts of the college campus. He also became an active supporter of the Los Angeles City College Foundation, an auxiliary organization dedicated to fundraising that created new enthusiasm on campus and in the community at large through funding of improvement projects. All of these actions helped change the image of the college and the attitudes of the once-forlorn campus population.

As the developer and the college continued to find successful solutions to issues, they gained a feeling of mutual trust and genuine respect. This was perhaps the single most important element in keeping the partnership together as it toiled to have the design approved through all the bureaucracies—the City of Los Angeles, the Los Angeles Community College District, the Department of State Architecture (DSA), and the college shared-governance process.

The original time line was only eighteen months but it was lengthened significantly for several reasons. First, a new concept design was inevitable because of the budget overrun and fire marshal requirements. To cut costs, the building was shortened, the width of the range was decreased, and a third level of tee boxes was added. The parking area was relocated to the side of the range to preclude having to add a fire sprinkler system. Another reason why the eighteen months dragged into four years was all of the other unforeseen bureaucratic steps that ensued. The project architect had to redesign the drawings and resubmit them to DSA, which had a minimum rework time of six months, which soon became a year. Each change also had to be reviewed by the district's facilities director and his team of experts. And because this was the first project of its kind, the board of trustees and the chancellor gave each change even more scrutiny and legal review than subsequent projects. Thus, the final challenge was to keep the developer interested in doing the project. Frequent, honest communications and great determination made this possible. The partners never gave up and were able to continue in their commitment because they had built a foundation of trust early on.

Just as the final plans were approved by DSA in April 2001, the Los Angeles Community College District's first-ever billion-dollar bond measure, Proposition A, was approved. This action provided $147 million for Los Angeles City College improvements, renovations, and dreams that were inconceivable in 1997. It also required a new look at whether or not the project should move forward or be revised. The master plan that was subsequently developed called for a new athletic zone on the south campus. The questions about what was now going to be a very densely used area were these: Did the driving range still fit? Did the design have to be modified? How best could the other elements be added—that is, a track, field, and stadium? The master planners recommended putting all of the parking under the field, similar to a design used at the University of California–Los Angeles. This would allow the two projects, the field-stadium complex and the driving range, to coexist and would create an even greater "new statement" about the college. Now the golf range project really fit into a bolder scheme of transformation of the college campus by creating a true athletic zone, along with the relocation of the physical education building, for the students and community.

Benefits and Outcomes for the Community College

In any successful deal the partners must ask, "What's in it for me?" In this case, the benefits to the developer have become fairly obvious. He receives a monetary return on his investment and increases his stature in his community. For the college there are several overt and many latent benefits resulting from the partnership. The following lists some of the positive outcomes for the college and the types of items that a public partner might want in ensuring a successful business outcome: improvement of a space at no cost; rental income; improved relations with the Korean community; green, grassy space instead of asphalt; a new marketing feature for the college; a way to "park" land for future use; added revenue from new golf classes; improved security on the south side of the campus; supplemental maintenance income; and an improved image in the larger community served.

Finally, this was the first new project that the college had undertaken in many years. By engaging in this innovative venture, the college leadership proved that the school could create new and brighter visions. The project served as a catalyst for new improvement on the campus and changed the culture so that people began to believe things can change for the better. In many ways, it is, therefore, a symbolic statement in addition to being a good business decision.

Conclusion

A community college is just like any business when it sets out to use one of the available economic models to accomplish its goals. Too often, though, opportunities pass it by because it is not ready. Community colleges, more than most other institutions, are ill prepared to respond to these business-driven, entrepreneurial opportunities because they are more risk-averse. Thus, they often lose the merits and benefits of economic partnerships. Whether the relationship is public-private or public-public, few community colleges have the experience necessary to use this mechanism for new growth or as a solution for their many challenges. Many also lack the creativity, will, or understanding of business to cut through the bureaucracy both in the institution and in other agencies needed to take advantage of an opportunity.

What remains unsaid about the project and the partnership is that it was one of the first actions that the college's new leadership undertook that enabled the change. Even though the process was tedious, the bold action to do something never tried before bore unexpected fruit by uniting the community and the college. Once united, the two parties were able to see possibilities for other partnerships and went on to initiate other activities. By being open to new ideas and taking a prudent risk that many faculty and administrators initially questioned, the administrative college leadership team was able to prove to the many nonbelievers that new initiatives were possible—like purchasing property for a new satellite campus and reopening the nursing program with the cooperation of three hospitals. Thus, the partnership awoke the sleeping cells of creativity that ultimately allowed the rebirth of the campus and its users.

It perhaps also reenergized the college staff and faculty to enable them to take an even bolder step—actively supporting the largest bond measure ever in California community college history. Mumford's (1952) suggestion about urban development clearly shows how powerful an integrated sense of community can be and how educational institutions must be a partner with business and community to be of value. This partnership is one example of how an opportunity can be developed and fuel even larger developments. Therefore, it is imperative not to let novel ideas die because of fear, intransigence, or impatience. Success can be achieved if there is commitment and will.

Reference

Mumford, L. "The Modern City." In T. Hamlin (ed.), *Forms and Functions of Twentieth-Century Architecture. Vol. 4: Building Types.* New York: Columbia University Press, 1952.

ARTHUR Q. TYLER is vice president of administrative services and budget at Los Angeles City College, California.

4

This nationally acclaimed partnership, built around an apprentice program and based on a foundation of trust and cooperation, illustrates how a trade union and a community college can find a way to use a mutual interest to benefit students and workers.

A Community College Partnership with an Electrical Contractor and Union

John P. Allen

Union and contractor representatives seek to upgrade and further legitimize the education and training of their apprentices and members by forming partnerships with educational institutions—in particular, community colleges. Union leaders and contractors see the need for and importance of preparing members to work in a rapidly changing world where work is becoming more sophisticated and complex. Members must have greater knowledge and a broader understanding of this shift to a more technical and interactive workplace. The emphasis in today's world of work is on people with education and training. Partnerships with community colleges allow union members to capitalize on the need for a better-educated and prepared workforce.

This chapter describes a partnership formed between an electrical contractor and a union and surrounding community colleges, the contractual agreement created to implement the partnership, the development of the curriculum, and the outcomes achieved by the partnership.

Formation of the Partnership

In 1998, Illinois Valley Community College (IVCC) entered into a unique partnership with the Joint Apprenticeship Training Committee (JATC) Local 176, which represents the National Electrical Contractors Association (NECA) and the International Brotherhood of Electrical Workers (IBEW Local Union 176). This partnership, one of the first of its kind in America, allows a Local 176 apprentice to take classes during a five-year apprenticeship period to earn an associate degree in electrical construction technology. The result is that the apprentice receives the degree at the same time he or she completes the training to become a registered journeyman.

The training director for Local 176 had approached Illinois Valley Community College earlier about the possibility of offering an associate degree in applied sciences (A.A.S.) in electrical construction technology for apprentices enrolled in the NECA and the IBEW union apprenticeship program in north central Illinois. Personnel from both Local 176 and the college attended this initial meeting.

The training director explained to the college representatives the union's ongoing efforts to raise the educational level of its electrical apprentices. The training director described the already-existing apprenticeship program: a five-year experience made up of eight thousand hours of on-the-job training in the electrical construction field under the direct supervision of a graduated, skilled journeyman electrician, in combination with a minimum of eight hundred hours of classroom schooling provided by experienced and competent journeyman electricians. These classes were taken one or two evenings a week throughout the year at a Local 176 center in Joliet, Illinois. The program was registered with the Bureau of Apprenticeship and Training at the U.S. Department of Labor and with the Veterans Administration.

The training director explained the vision of Local 176 to allow the graduates of its apprenticeship program to receive their two-year degree at the same time they achieved journeyman status. A similar associate degree program developed for the NECA-IBEW union electrical apprentices already existed in Indiana. Based on the information supplied to the college representatives, the college made a commitment to the Local 176 representatives that it would study the feasibility of developing the A.A.S. degree in electrical construction technology for Local 176.

Community College Collaboration

The process of developing the program turned out to be complex. First, the territory covered by Local 176 was extensive, including four different public community colleges: Illinois Valley Community College (IVCC), Kankakee Community College, Black Hawk College, and Joliet Junior College. Therefore, an agreement to work together on this matter, including letters of support to IVCC from the other colleges, was required before the project could move forward. These letters of commitment and support were received after it was agreed that each community college would be able to offer the general education courses required for completion of the A.A.S. degree.

Another complicating factor was that although IVCC would award the degree to the apprentices, the technical core, the internship, and related courses would be taught by Local 176 at its training center, which is located in the Joliet Junior College district. Therefore, Joliet Junior College had to give permission to IVCC to offer courses and the A.A.S. degree under rules and regulations established by the governing board for Illinois public community colleges. Joliet Junior College granted this approval.

Another matter to be worked out before the Illinois Community College Board and the Illinois Board of Higher Education (IBHE) would give the program their approval was the commitment by Local 176 that the A.A.S. degree would be open to all citizens without regard for sex, race, creed, and so on, and that no discriminatory actions would be taken that violated any state and federal legislation on nondiscriminatory practices. After lengthy discussions and correspondence between IVCC, ICCB, and IBHE representatives, all parties came to a mutual understanding and agreement on admission of students and control exerted by IVCC in regulating and monitoring admission into the program. A written agreement between IVCC and JATC Local 176 was developed and approved to the satisfaction of ICCB and IBHE allowing for admission of students into the program. Today, Local 176 retains direct control over admission of students into their program as long as these admission regulations are observed.

Contractual Agreement

In 1998, IVCC and JATC Local 176 entered into a contractual cooperative agreement—a joint effort between the two parties to work in collaboration to develop and offer an A.A.S. degree in electrical construction technology to the apprentices in the NECA-IBEW. The curriculum consists of 65.5 credit hours. IVCC evaluates the electrician apprenticeship program in accordance with its own practices and the requirements of the Illinois Community College Board.

The technical core and elective courses are taught by the Local 176 teachers, who are referred to and hired by IVCC after meeting IVCC's hiring requirements. The general education courses are taught by IVCC and the other community colleges included in the agreement. The internship courses are provided under the direction and guidance of a Local 176 journeyman on the job. IVCC pays the Local 176 instructors at the prevailing front-line supervisor pay rate, with Local 176 picking up any related mileage costs incurred by these instructors to teach these courses.

The college and Local 176 agreed that applicants selected for the program must meet requirements based on standards registered by the Bureau of Apprenticeship and Training at the U.S. Department of Labor. These requirements are as follows: the applicant must be a high school graduate or have a general education diploma at the time of the application period, be at least eighteen years old at the time of the application period, have taken two semesters of high school or college algebra with a minimum C grade in each semester completed at the time of application period, be a resident of the jurisdiction of Local 176 for one year, have acceptable physical health as determined by a physician to be able to perform the tasks of a construction electrician safely, including drug testing, and have evidence of a qualifying grade on an aptitude test as prescribed in the registered standards. The standards encompass IVCC admissions requirements and Local 176 eligibility requirements. The college enrolls into the A.A.S. electrician construction technology program those applicants meeting these selection criteria for both the college and Local 176.

Apprentices enrolling in the general education courses at IVCC, Kankakee Community College, Black Hawk College, and Joliet Junior College are charged applicable tuition and fees for the courses. Local 176 reimburses the enrolled apprentices for tuition and fees upon completion of the general education courses with a minimum grade of C in each course. The apprentices are responsible for the textbook charges.

Local 176 reimburses IVCC for the amount of gross pay, including withholding and payroll taxes, for the electrician construction technology instructors employed to teach in this program. Local 176 also pays a one-time fee of $17.50 to IVCC for each faculty member it employs to cover the cost of a criminal background check. Local 176 pays the college 15 percent of the total amount of the contract to cover additional administrative costs incurred by the college for handling personnel, student registration, and records management.

Each party insures against all losses and damages that are the result of the fault or negligence of that party in carrying out its obligations and services of the agreement, including general liability insurance. Each party provides a certificate of insurance showing that the necessary coverage is in force and naming the other party to the agreement, their officers, and employees as additional named insureds. Each party provides thirty days' written notice before the insurance is modified or cancelled.

This contractual agreement between IVCC and JATC Local 176 officially began on October 5, 1998, and automatically renews for one year on the anniversary date until such time as the agreement is terminated.

Curriculum Development

The curriculum for the A.A.S. degree program consists of 38 credit hours of technical or core courses: Basic Industrial Electricity I & II, Motors and Controls I & II, Programmable Logic Control I & II, Electrical Wiring, Introduction to Electronics, Beginning Industrial Electronics, Solid State Electronics, Industrial Instrumentation, Instruments & Measurements, and Machine Blueprint Reading. There are also 10 credit hours of internship or on-the-job experience, 2.5 credit hours of related elective courses, including safety, cardiopulmonary resuscitation, and welding, and 15 credit hours of general education courses. The general education courses are these: History of the Labor Movement, Oral Communications, Written

Communications, Human Relations in the World of Work, and Technical Mathematics. As noted earlier, the total program is 65.5 credit hours. The technical or core courses were approved by the American Council on Education. In addition, IVCC's electronics-electrician instructor determined that the course content was comparable to the courses offered by the college. IVCC hires the Local 176 instructors on a part-time basis to teach these technical and related courses at the Joliet training center.

All four community colleges offer the general education courses to allow apprentices living in their districts to complete the general education component of the degree. However, the degree itself is awarded by IVCC to all graduating students.

IVCC developed and put together the form required by the Illinois Community College Board and the Illinois Board of Higher Education to get approval by the state to offer certificate and degree programs. The college submitting the application for approval of a certificate or degree program must conduct a needs assessment that includes supply and demand, labor market information, student interest, required curriculum, instructional needs, equipment, facility and supply needs, and partnership and articulation agreements. The form is an extensive and involved document that must contain all the relevant data and materials required by Illinois Community College Board and Illinois Board of Higher Education before the college receives final approval to offer the program.

Partnership Outcomes

IVCC received approval to offer the A.A.S. degree in electrical construction technology in 1999. Local 176 then began enrolling apprentices into the courses. As already noted, Local 176 traditionally had a night program that took five years, with the apprentices attending classes several evenings a week and working during the day. In 1999, Local 176 worked with the college to enroll approximately sixty apprentices in courses leading to the A.A.S. degree program.

By summer 2000, Local 176 initiated a new daytime apprentice program with another doubling of the number of apprentices enrolled in coursework at the college. The enrollment statistics for the year 2001 showed the college was serving approximately three hundred apprentices in the new degree program. When these individuals earn their A.A.S. degrees, they will be better educated, better prepared to meet the needs of employers, and better qualified to make career choices that allow for promotions in the electronics-electrical field. They can become front-line supervisors, estimators, superintendents on the job, or even contractors owning their own business.

As noted earlier, the program is supported financially by contributions from Local 176 for expenses related to the offering of courses and services to Local 176 and by state appropriations for apprentices enrolled in the courses. The partnership is a win-win situation; both organizations benefit from the relationship. Local 176 has a high-quality educational program that is accredited and available on-site to apprentices. The college increases its enrollment and gains additional state appropriation dollars to maintain and improve its offerings in general. As a result, the college can better serve the citizens of the district who are seeking educational opportunities.

The college is currently working on forming partnerships with other contractor and union organizations to provide high standards and high-quality educational offerings to apprentices. In the meantime, the goal of the Local 176/college partnership is to require an A.A.S. degree for entry-level journeymen.

Conclusion

Even though there were many obstacles to overcome in forming this partnership, IVCC and JATC Local 176 representatives always kept in mind the need to serve the students and citizens of their district. Some challenges that had to be addressed included overcoming a natural reluctance to change from traditional ways of doing business, taking the necessary steps to make a commitment by both parties to work collaboratively, and charting new waters to implement a new partnership that serves as a model in forming working relationships between community colleges and unions. The people involved in forming the partnership exhibited patience, perseverance, and cohesiveness in keeping the goal in mind. These people would not take no for an answer, and they continued to work together to achieve the objective. The partnership is built on a solid foundation of trust and cooperation and continues to flourish to the benefit of all parties.

This type of partnership can be and is being developed elsewhere between community colleges and unions. IVCC has received numerous requests for information about the partnership from other community colleges around the country. In the state of Illinois alone, IVCC has worked with six or seven other community colleges to supply information and advice about this partnership. IBEW and NECA have affiliations around the country where partnerships of this nature could be developed and implemented.

John P. Allen is associate vice president of academic affairs at Illinois Valley Community College.

5

A partnership of public agencies and small, private sector manufacturers squarely confronts the challenge of educating men and women in the field of manufacturing technology.

Asnuntuck Community College's Machine Technology Certificate and Degree Programs

Harvey S. Irlen, Frank D. Gulluni

Manufacturing, a traditional source of employment throughout Connecticut, continues to experience skills shortages in the workforce. Despite overall job losses in the last decade, manufacturing remains a strong sector in Connecticut and offers high wages and benefits. Productivity has been greatly enhanced by technology, but virtually all manufacturers cite lack of skilled workers as their greatest barrier to growth. Specifically, critical shortages exist in the area of precision machining and are confirmed consistently by data from a wide variety of sources, including the Connecticut Department of Labor (DOL), the Capitol Region Workforce Development Board, manufacturing associations, individual firms, and other state, public, and private sector agencies.

The hourly pay rate for metal machining personnel averages more than $15.00, and most employers provide full-time employment with overtime and excellent fringe benefit packages. A recent review of machining positions in Connecticut's job bank listed 790 openings. Connecticut has a diversified and dynamic manufacturing core but an aging workforce; consequently, the need for technology education and training is obvious and dramatic.

The future of manufacturing in Connecticut, whether in photonics, metal machining, aerospace products, or electronics, depends largely on education and a collective ability to influence two constituencies: eighteen-to twenty-two-year-olds who will be entering the workforce and incumbent workers who have been employed for any number of years.

This chapter describes the formation and growth of a partnership between several public agencies and small manufacturers in north central Connecticut. The potential benefits of proximity—Connecticut is a very small state—were sharpened by the manufacturers' urgent need for skilled employees. A description of the setting and the players will be followed by a discussion of the program and curriculum, a look at early results, and an indication of short- and long-term benefits to businesses and communities alike.

Program Purpose: The Partners

The origins of what is now the Asnuntuck Community College Manufacturing Technology Center can be traced back to 1996 and a group of interested parties in the greater Enfield community: the North Central Connecticut Chamber of Commerce; town officials, including the mayor, town manager, town council, and director of economic development; Asnuntuck Community College officials; and local manufacturers. Their collective objective was to identify methods through which employers could fill significant numbers of openings in the metal machining classifications. The group met regularly for more than a year to identify the necessary components of such an effort. Key among these was the need to educate high school parents, students, and counselors about the realities of contemporary manufacturing. Equally important was the need to enhance and upgrade the skills of current employees so they could advance their own careers by moving into higher-level positions, thereby creating openings in entry-level positions that would help establish career ladders for new employees.

Partnership Development

In September 1997, the group engaged a consultant who, within a few weeks, developed a proposal for the establishment and funding of a machine technology start-up effort at Asnuntuck Community College. Because no pool of money was readily available for the group's specific objective—funding for staffing and capital equipment—the college sought the assistance of local and state elected officials. Their collective recommendation was to pursue funding through the Connecticut Department of Economic and Community Development (DECD). DECD usually provides dollars directly to the private sector as part of incentive packages for capital enhancement, primarily for building expansion and new equipment. It is highly unusual for this funding agent to provide training dollars to a public agency. Nonetheless, largely because of the very effective support of the manufacturing sector in the greater Hartford community, DECD made an allocation of $500,000. Groups ranging from the Hartford Growth Council, East of the River Chambers of Commerce, and the North Central Chamber continued actively to trumpet the need for training and retraining, especially in the areas of precision machining.

The college also was able to use a study that had been commissioned in 1995 by the Hartford Growth Council to determine the level of need for new employees in precision machining, as well as the requirements for upgrading the incumbent workforce. The study, conducted by a regional consulting group, identified gaps in the preparation of both new workers and incumbent workers and also identified the serious absence of training providers.

In reality, Asnuntuck and its local supporters had before them a fairly direct and well-developed pathway to an important funding source. The needs assessments had been completed and the synergy established among the partners. Together with Asnuntuck's willingness to take the leadership role in the implementation of a precision machining program, these proved to be an ideal combination for success with DECD.

Another important idea that had to be considered when seeking government assistance was replicability. The college wanted to demonstrate clearly both its ability and willingness to share and to help other agencies implement similar programming. Through its expanding relationship with the Hartford Growth Council and continuing advocacy from the board of trustees and the chancellor of the community college system, Asnuntuck sought to forge partnerships with other community colleges that wished to offer some courses or the entire precision machining program.

In short, the college presented real needs; established meaningful partnerships with corporate, community, and public officials; developed a proposal that was clear and concise about its goals, objectives, and outcomes; and finally, demonstrated both the ability and the desire to assist other agencies to develop similar coursework and programs. In December 1997 Asnuntuck was notified that DECD would fund the program for a period of one year. Immediately, the group began the process of identifying machining-related tooling and materials and defining space requirements at the college.[1]

During the period from December 8, 1997, to March 1, 1998, with assistance from its private sector mentors, Asnuntuck's accomplishments included the following:

- It established an advisory board of manufacturing representatives to assist with final selection of students and approval of curriculum, machinery, and the physical environment.
- It began the renovation process of six thousand square feet of space at the college.
- It instituted a search for instructors and other staff.
- It located sufficient equipment at Pratt & Whitney, Hamilton Sundstrand (then Hamilton Standard), ABB/Combustion Engineering, and other local companies.
- It purchased appropriate and necessary supplies and materials for use by students and staff.

- It developed curriculum and identified textbooks, workbooks, and other instructional materials.
- It marketed the program to the general public and to the Connecticut and Massachusetts workforce development systems.
- It provided orientation for and assessed over one hundred candidates for sixty openings, thirty each in a day program and an evening program.
- In 1998, it started the programs officially on February 29 (day program) and March 1 (evening program).

At approximately the same time the Asnuntuck program was being established—and in response to the same statewide need for entry-level machine operators and higher-level technical skills for both new entrants and incumbents—more than a dozen employers in the aerospace industry formed Aerospace Components Manufacturers (ACM). Immediately afterward, they developed and disseminated bid packages to purchase training for their core employees. In addition, individual employers, like CUNO, Inc., a manufacturer of filter systems in Enfield, reached out to local and state government seeking ways and means to identify new employees and to upgrade those whom they already employed.

CUNO, in fact, made clear to Enfield officials that its primary consideration in determining whether to expand locally or elsewhere nationally or internationally was, quite simply, *workforce development*. Consequently, the town requested assistance from Asnuntuck Community College to establish immediate and long-term educational plans and coursework for all levels of employees at CUNO, ranging from the assembler to engineers and managers. In a two-year effort to assist CUNO's growth and technology development, Asnuntuck provided coursework for more than two hundred employees, with subjects ranging from English as a second language to advanced mathematics and statistical process control.

Asnuntuck's commitment to the combination of manufacturing technology and higher education, demonstrated through the machine technology certificate and degree programs, proved to be of critical importance to the agencies that partnered in a successful effort to retain and expand CUNO in Enfield: the town of Enfield, DECD and DOL, and CUNO itself.

The college has also reached out to its sister institutions across the state. This effort, in turn, has led to numerous relationships and partnerships. Among these are chambers of commerce; state, city, and town economic development boards; manufacturing groups like ACM and the Connecticut Tooling and Machining Association; DECD; college advisory boards; and scores of employers who have been willing to provide students with internships, mentoring, and eventually career opportunities.

The manufacturers with which the college is involved contribute time and effort, equipment and materials, internships, mentoring, plant tours, and cash, especially for students who require tooling and related materials and supplies. Of equal importance, the college has obtained workforce development matching funds of more than $2 million from the Governor's Office for Workforce Competitiveness, DOL's customized job training program, and DECD.

The internship program in particular has proven invaluable, especially for student self-development. The students have been able to use the internship component to demonstrate skills learned, identify areas in which they need to put more energy, and develop their self-confidence. It also provides affirmation that students have made the right choice in pursuing a precision machining course of study. At the same time, the employer community is able to use this relationship to convey to the interns that they are integral to the future of manufacturing in Connecticut.

Internships are conducted frequently in two phases. In the early stages of the first semester, students participate with a manufacturing company in a "shadowing" or observation capacity to gain a better perspective of the labor market and observe the diversity of skills and abilities that are required by the industry. They are provided a follow-up experience with the same employer in the second semester. At this point, participants usually are able to function independently and "show" the employer how they have progressed both personally and technologically. Each internship is scheduled for a one-week time frame, and the employer is required to provide a written report on attendance, attitude, and ability.

As stated previously, the private sector commitment to a project or program is the most important ingredient to both funding success and the long-term sustained effort. In pursuing funding from a variety of state agencies for the machine technology program, the college was required to demonstrate the overall dollar value of the private sector's commitment. The contributions ranged from machinery and tooling to internships, technical assistance, and payment to incumbent workers who participate in related coursework.

Without the full support and involvement of the private sector, technology programs can survive and exist. But with private sector commitment and immersion in the overall and continuing effort, a program will flourish. Of equal importance, an environment of openness and participation involving all relevant parties will surely lead to the development of other technology programs and coursework. This has been the experience at Asnuntuck. The college's list of courses and programs in technology has grown enormously and now includes electricity, pneumatics, hydraulics, welding, lean manufacturing, team building, problem solving, computer numerical control, and computer assisted manufacturing.

The manufacturing technology center is guided in its efforts by input from an advisory committee, which includes representatives of the business community, economic development officials, and human resource development professionals. In establishing this committee, the college recruited employer representatives from a mix of industries and localities to ensure broad-based representation. The advisory committee in many ways is the conscience of the center. The college needs to concentrate on curriculum design, interagency agreements, budgets, staffing, student development, and other aspects of the center's operation. The advisory committee speaks for the customer, a constant reminder that no matter how well run, the center will be effective only if it serves the employer community and the student population competently.

Program Curriculum and Expansion

As the core machining program was being implemented in 1998, college officials and their growing partnership of public agencies, chambers of commerce, other community colleges, economic development officials, and especially, private sector representatives also began efforts to upgrade curriculum and coursework to degree-level status. On the one hand, college credit would ensure inclusion of those in the community who were seeking two- or four-year degrees in various areas of manufacturing technology. On the other hand, though, such activity would almost certainly exclude significant numbers of youth and adults in the population who either were not prepared to participate in a two-year degree-granting process or were seeking entry-level employment in technological fields.

The solution was to develop a four-part machining-manufacturing technology program that was almost totally inclusive, and yet at the same time reflected the needs of the employer community and respected the integrity of higher education. Although the plan is fairly simple and straightforward, apparently no other program serves the needs of students through such a four-level technology cluster as described here.

Level One (Original Core Program). This is a 780-hour entry-level machining program featuring mathematics, blueprint reading, introductory CNC, and manual machining skills and theory (twelve college credits).

Students who complete Level One have the following options: related employment, related employment and part-time enrollment in Level Two, full-time Level Two enrollment and part-time employment, and machinist apprenticeship through DOL.

Level Two. This is a one-year certificate program including Level One coursework plus advanced mathematics, engineering drawing, CNC, and CAM (thirty college credits). Students who complete Level Two have the following options: career machining employment and part-time enrollment in Level Three, full-time Level Three enrollment and part-time employment, and machinist apprenticeship through DOL.

Level Three. Level Three includes previously described coursework plus required studies and electives for an associate degree in manufacturing technology (sixty-six college credits). Students who complete Level Three have at a minimum the following options: career employment and opportunity to matriculate to Central Connecticut State University as third-year students attending full-time or part-time.

Level Four. Level Four is third-year status in the College of Technology at Central Connecticut State University. The Asnuntuck curriculum is competency-based and aligned with standards established by the National Tooling and Machining Association and Connecticut's Board of Governors for Higher Education. A private sector technical-education committee will test students as part of an arrangement with the National Institute for Metalworking Systems, a national credentialing agency representing manufacturing corporations, technical schools and colleges, and labor organizations. Skills standards are of utmost importance to the students, the employer community, and the community college system. An external evaluation using national technology standards provides further knowledge about students' levels of achievement as well as Asnuntuck's capacity to ensure a professional learning environment.

The target population includes men and women ages eighteen to sixty-plus with educational levels ranging from high school to college. Some have language limitations. Work histories range from zero to more than thirty years. Employment status ranges from those who are presently underemployed or minimum-wage earners to those who have been dislocated from the workforce for periods of a few weeks to many months; usually, they are people seeking new and upgraded careers. Previous occupations range from the unskilled transferring from work site to work site every few months to those who have worked in assembly, maintenance, basic manufacturing, offices, and service industries. The population so described includes thousands of youth and adults across the state of Connecticut: incumbent workers, dislocated workers, women in transition, underemployed persons, and recent high school graduates.

Asnuntuck's internal evaluation system collects and analyzes data in order to facilitate continuous quality improvement. The fundamental plan-do-check-act sequence of TQM provides a framework for a process that includes identifying and tracking employment, labor market trends, and related customer needs. The mix of services, courses, and performance measures is refined through customer feedback, and this ongoing communication allows the program ultimately to focus on performance and value-added outcomes like return on investment.

Student Outcomes

Asnuntuck's machine technology program was chosen by the Connecticut Economic Development Association as the number one new program in the state in 1998.

The first class graduated from the program in August 1998; there were twenty-eight students. More than 90 percent accepted related employment before or at the close of the program activities. The evening students graduated in December, having completed the core 780-hour program over the extended period of forty-two weeks. Again, there were twenty-eight graduates, and placements and upgrades occurred for more than 90 percent of them. During the month of September, a second day program with thirty-six students was started. That group graduated in April 1999, and thirty-two of the graduates accepted upgrades and employment in the manufacturing sector in Connecticut.

Currency and Relevance. A principal result of involving the private sector from the planning stages has been the emphasis on currency and relevance for the program and the students. New technology is constantly being introduced in the private sector; consequently, it is incumbent on the training provider to make sure that the students gain the education as well as the technical skills to allow them to make a successful transition to the private sector. Many technical programs discount the educational preparation required for graduates to succeed in the long term in the private sector. Asnuntuck's experience in education, together with the mandates of the community college system in Connecticut, dictate the emphasis on academic instruction and the addition of computer skills as integral components of any technology preparation, especially one so challenging as the machining industry.

Options. The program design provides students with options. At any level in the career ladder, there is an assurance of viable, well-paid employment upon completion and the opportunity for the individual to return to an educational setting at some point in the future. Using this unique program design, Asnuntuck has an impact on youth and adults, men and women, economically advantaged and disadvantaged people, and others in the population who are underrepresented. More important than simply serving these populations are the critical outputs: *retention, completion, career.*

Motivation. Student motivation here is no different from other community college programs in which students are determined to graduate and transfer to four-year degree programs. Once a student learns to develop new skills and abilities, he or she usually wants more. Also, each step in the program means more money, benefits, and career latitude in the private sector. The great percentage of students who enroll with the thought of completing Levels One or Two will continue full-time or part-time and achieve Level Three status, and perhaps even Level Four. This type of incremental programming has the greatest potential for short- and long-term success. The student can see the end result; once it is achieved, he or she can aim higher.

Benefits to State, Local Communities, and the Private Sector

At the risk of sounding repetitious, it may be appropriate to gather in one place a list of the beneficial results of this program. Some were intended, some were simply serendipitous, most were the product of the dedication and commitment of employers and public servants who knew that manufacturing in Connecticut was far from dead and that a vibrant workforce was available and ready for the training:

- Long-term relationships are formed between education and economic development.
- Industry is expanded and retained in the region.
- Participants' academic skills and technical abilities are improved to ensure a more successful employment experience.
- There is greater participation by industry in the development of internship, mentorship, entrepreneurship, and summer job programs for the in-school population.
- There are increased numbers of entry-level positions for the unemployed and underemployed.
- The Asnuntuck model has been replicated in other community colleges and technology clusters.
- Academic and technology skills development is available to diverse populations.
- The model is a marketing tool for state and local economic development initiatives.
- Community colleges become external providers of education and training, frequently to firms and industries that have shut down their own training departments.
- Linkages in the private-public sector relationship are strengthened.
- Technology and academic options are enhanced for incumbent workers.
- The technology clusters are flexible enough to ensure that participants, including incumbent workers, can enter and exit at any level.
- Greater numbers of people are included in postsecondary education.
- There is the ability to access other funding for the expansion of workforce development in a continuing and critical effort to sustain and expand the local manufacturing base.

Conclusion

Government, industry, community colleges, school systems, labor organizations, chambers of commerce, and local communities—together—need to establish new and additional programs and networks to make an impact on business and industry and upgrade the skills and abilities of the incumbent worker, the unemployed and underemployed, the school dropout population, and the high school students and graduates who are uncertain about their future, the workplace, and their role in postsecondary education. It is imperative that community colleges continue to develop a comprehensive preparatory system that integrates education and employment and for which continuous learning and quality improvement are the norm. The foundation for such an approach to educational development, partnering with local businesses and the community, is in place at Asnuntuck Community College.

Note

1. In the fall of 1997, Asnuntuck agreed to participate in a concurrent effort to obtain private funding for the establishment of similar programs at the community colleges in Hartford and Manchester, Connecticut. Though some funding was eventually secured, the resulting programs were not as robust as the Asnuntuck program. The programs at other schools remained somewhat marginal until 2000, when the Asnuntuck-led Precision Manufacturing Institute was created using funds from a DECD grant that included equipment money for other colleges interested in establishing machine technology programs.

HARVEY S. IRLEN *is president of Asnuntuck Community College, Connecticut.*

FRANK D. GULLUNI *is director of the machine technology center at Asnuntuck Community College, Connecticut.*

6

A community-college-and-industry-based partnership formed in response to a large public works project in a depressed region of Los Angeles County faced the challenges of developing an outreach and career-path program for hard-to-serve clients in a short time span.

The Alameda Corridor Industry & College Collaborative

Lou Anne Bynum

This chapter discusses the development and implementation of a comprehensive college-and-industry-based training partnership. The chapter begins with a description of how the Alameda Corridor Industry & College Collaborative came to be and its essential charge. It then describes the partnership's operational and administrative structure, identifies basic components of the project, and outlines the many challenges faced in implementing the project and meeting mandated outcomes. The chapter describes the partners involved, the challenges of project administration, and the project results, and concludes with core participant outcomes and lessons learned for the eight-member college consortium.

Description of the Project

The Alameda Corridor Industry & College Collaborative, a workforce development consortium of eight community colleges, was established in 1998 through a series of California Community College Chancellor's Office economic development grants totaling $1.6 million. In response to a $2.4 billion public works consolidated rail construction project extending from the ports of Long Beach and Los Angeles to East Los Angeles, and in anticipation of the creation of ten thousand construction- and trades-related jobs locally (Alameda Corridor Transportation Authority, 1999), the consortium members came together to address the workforce training needs of the under- and unemployed residents of the area surrounding the twenty-mile construction project. The Gateway Cities region, consisting of twenty-seven

NEW DIRECTIONS FOR COMMUNITY COLLEGES, no. 119, Fall 2002 © Wiley Periodicals, Inc.

cities from Long Beach to East Los Angeles that surround and border the construction project, is one of the most severely economically depressed regions of Los Angeles County.

Mission

The mission of the Alameda Corridor Industry & College Collaborative was to "provide state-of-the-art, industry-driven trade and technical training through the community college partnership, which prepares local residents for jobs in the region's critical industries" (Alameda Corridor Industry & College Collaborative, 1998, p. 1). To that end, the collaborative built a consortium and strategic partnership including eight community colleges, industry, and public and private organizations in the region. Through links with local agencies and numerous community-based organizations, the collaborative initially identified residents for training and new job opportunities on the construction project. In addition, the collaborative identified the training needs of employers in the region and targeted the local workforce for skills upgrading and entry-level jobs in key industry clusters, including transportation, construction, manufacturing-aerospace, and environmental mitigation ("Project Paints Picture of Teamwork," 2001).

Structure of the Collaborative

The collaborative consisted of eight regional community colleges located in and around the Gateway Cities region of Los Angeles County. Long Beach City College developed the concept, wrote the grants, and served as the lead and administrative agent. Other partners included Gateway Cities Partnership Inc., a regional economic development organization including twenty-seven municipalities in southeast Los Angeles County, the Alameda Corridor Jobs Coalition, the Alameda Corridor Transit Authority, local employment development departments, and regional private industry councils.

Project Management Team. The management team, which was employed by Long Beach City College, had offices at Gateway Cities Partnership in Paramount. The team included a project director, operations manager, workforce career advisers, and industry consultants.

Steering Committee. The steering committee met monthly. The economic development and occupational education deans from the eight colleges who were on the team provided direction, set policy, and monitored performance outcomes. Contributing participants also included college welfare-to-work directors, community-based job development organizations, and representatives of the region's private industry councils.

Technical Assistance–Industry Advisory Committees. Technical assistance committees, made up of faculty and industry experts, advised on the type of training and curricula needed. Industry advisory committees shared information about employer-training needs, determined required skill sets and proficiency levels, and developed internships and job links for students.

Project Components

The $1.6 million in grants awarded for this training project allowed for an eighteen-month performance delivery time line. Key objectives included outreach and recruitment to train four hundred people, of which 50 percent were to be welfare recipients. The project had an initial goal of placing approximately 50 percent of the total trained into entry-level jobs.

The construction project coordinated by the Alameda Corridor Transportation Authority (ACTA) was expected to bring ten thousand new jobs in construction to the region, and later, fifty thousand new jobs to California because of the improved rail transportation link. The construction contractor was required by regional cities and funding agencies to train 1,000 local residents in construction and related fields and hire 30 percent of the graduates for the construction project. The goal was to provide 650 people with preapprenticeship training and 350 with nontrades training. ACTA contracted with the Alameda Corridor Jobs Coalition, a public-private coalition of community-based organizations, to direct outreach efforts and identify area residents to work on the project and receive the necessary training.

The challenge was that over five thousand residents expressed interest in the one thousand training spots offered. Residents who had some job-readiness skills and previous employment experience were selected for the preapprenticeship training spots. Of the remaining interested residents, most had some level of hardship and many had significant barriers to accessing immediate job-training opportunities.

Participant Characteristics

Although the rebounding economy in Los Angeles County has seen progress in the creation of jobs in select areas and industries, the corridor passes through communities that still struggle with welfare dependency, high unemployment, underemployment, and generally low incomes.

Economic Profile. A report prepared by the USC Center for Economic Development (2001) detailed the problems in the corridor cities. This area is home to 1.7 million people, or almost 18 percent of the population of Los Angeles County. Twenty-nine percent of the county's displaced aerospace workers and nearly 30 percent of all manufacturing jobs that disappeared in the county between 1994 and 1998 were in the corridor region. Despite a strong economy in 1999, and although unemployment rates varied greatly in the Gateway Cities region, the area had nearly twice the Los Angeles County unemployment rate of 5.86 percent (USC Center for Economic Development, 2001).

Ethnicity. The Gateway Cities region during the 1990s saw an increase in the immigrant population, led by a growing number of Hispanics. The region is a majority nonwhite area with most significant populations groups consisting of a Hispanic majority (54 percent), followed by non-Hispanic white (25 percent), Asian and Pacific Islander (11 percent), and African American (9 percent). In 1999, nearly 45 percent of the labor force of the Long Beach metropolitan area was foreign-born (Fogg and Harrington, 2001). Forty-three percent of the population in the Gateway region is under the age of twenty-four, compared with 36 percent in Los Angeles County and 35 percent in California overall. In addition, 35 percent of the population in the region had less than a high school education, compared with 30 percent and 24 percent in Los Angeles County and California, respectively (USC Center for Economic Development, 2001).

These changing demographics have significant implications for the current and future competitiveness of the labor force in the Gateway Cities region. High unemployment, a large immigrant population that lacks sufficient workplace skills and struggles with language and access barriers, high dropout rates, and a growing young population present immense challenges to the region and its ability to be competitive and attract high-wage jobs.

"Hard-to-Serve" Clients. Because of the relatively strong economy in Southern California over the past six years, people with even minimal skills have been able to find work. This leaves a challenging population as the target for skill-based vocational training. This population lacks not only technical skills but also the most basic work-preparedness and life skills that many other people take for granted. Many project participants had significant barriers—such as a history of under- and unemployment, low educational level, domestic and substance abuse problems—and many were single parents with child care and transportation problems. Many also were immigrants whose primary language was not English. It became clear at the outset that the hard-to-serve were the largest segment of people needing help.

To break the cycle of poverty and connect clients served in the collaborative to entry-level career-path jobs that would enable them to support a family above the poverty level, comprehensive assessment and support services were needed so that participants could reach the level of preparedness necessary for technical training.

The collaborative took a "career-ladder" approach in its outreach and provision of support services and training. Consequently, the initial goal of training four hundred residents, of whom 50 percent would be welfare recipients, in an eighteen-month time frame, was immediately reevaluated once the project got under way. Staffing was strategically reorganized not only around training and job placement but also around career-ladder orientation and support services so participants could access and receive assessment services. Advising and support services were critical in preparing participants for technical training success. The collaborative also realized that the original goal of placing 50 percent of those enrolled in training courses quickly into jobs was unrealistic.

Unrealistic Expectations. Because of the enormous scope of the construction project and the anticipated impact on the community, a high level of promotional visibility and promise of jobs associated with the project led to a heightened expectation among the local population that jobs would be immediate and plentiful. As already noted, five thousand people showed up at project job intake sites expressing interest in employment. Of these, approximately one thousand had the minimum basic skills required to take the tests that screened for the 650 apprenticeship positions. Expectations were exceedingly high, but in actuality, availability of immediate jobs was very low.

Innovative Outreach Strategies. The collaborative, already working in short time constraints, had a difficult time getting started in recruitment and outreach. The staff worked with community-based organizations to provide information about opportunities for training and job support services through the colleges. They soon discovered, however, that people at the standard outreach sites seeking work were impatient, disenchanted, and frustrated with the process and the promise of jobs. Many had simply given up any hope for employment and had quit looking for work. Others viewed training simply as "income loss." Those who had jobs needed to keep them; those who were unemployed were resistant to entering training programs—they wanted jobs. Innovative outreach strategies were required if the collaborative was to reach the people who needed help the most and convince them that good jobs were possible through the community college programs.

Collaborative staff fanned out to community churches, Laundromats, check-cashing centers, and street corners where people gathered and waited for day jobs. Given the diversity of the region and the high percentage of residents who did not speak English, bilingual staff were hired to go into the communities and distribute information and print materials in several languages. In addition to direct outreach, the collaborative created two recruitment videos to share with community-based organizations and scheduled the videos and public service announcements on twelve different networks (including Spanish-language stations) for six weeks, reaching eighty-one thousand households. These strategies had immediate success and helped the collaborative reach greater numbers of people more effectively and in a shorter period of time.

Project Challenges: Collaborative Partners

The Alameda Corridor Industry & College Collaborative was a large project, involving many partners operating in a short delivery time frame and requiring very specific outcomes in training and job placement. Because the project was funded as a California Community Colleges ED>Net (Economic Development Network) grant, statutory requirements dictated that programs and services "shall be demand-driven, delivery structures shall be agile, performance-oriented, cost-effective. . . . and shall include a strong partnership with local economic development entities, community-based organizations and the private sector" (California Community Colleges Chancellor's Office, 1998, p. 6).

From the standpoint of policy and governance, these requirements are appropriate and commendable; from a practical operational standpoint, they presented immense challenges. The collaborative commenced with six member colleges and added two more during the first few months. Community-based and local government partners stretched along the twenty-mile corridor from Long Beach in the South Bay area to East Los Angeles. The collaborative grants initially targeted four key industry clusters with each requiring business advisory partners. The administration of six grants to fund the collaborative included a set of terms and conditions for each, which required careful budget, audit, and operational oversight. And the monitoring, tracking, and reporting of data and outcomes stressed administrative support and systems.

Eight-Member College Consortium. The colleges came together at the request of the California Community Colleges Chancellor's Office through an inquiry from local state legislators who encouraged community college involvement. Economic development funds were identified through six ED>Net-funded grants. Economic development staff at Long Beach City College, who had prior experience in developing a workforce response model for an aerospace industry consortium, offered to develop the concept and write and administer the project.

The organizational structure of the collaborative project was created to include the project management and staff, the steering committee, the technical assistance committees, and business advisory groups to address issues related to job skills and employee training needs.

Through the steering committee, the colleges immediately and forthrightly determined policy, managed budgets, assigned tasks, maintained project accountability, and addressed territoriality issues. Two additional colleges in the area expressed interest and were included in the consortium. Foundations set by the steering committee allowed for equal input and equal access to available funds so each college could respond locally with those programs best suited to meet the training needs of the project's target industries. A "minigrant" process was developed, which required members to submit proposals for funds to deliver training and services locally. As a result, the eight colleges were able to offer a wide range of courses and support services to residents throughout the region. Courses were redesigned or newly developed in machinist training, manufacturing technology, auto emissions testing, introduction to five trades, machine tool operating, and automotive parts and servicing. There was also a miniproject focusing on accessing the Los Angeles colleges' trades programs.

Surprisingly, the most difficult step in working with the eight-college consortium was not the anticipated issues of budgeting and territoriality. Instead, the local business practices employed by each college were what hindered and slowed down the process. The operational transactions to process the various service and personnel contracts required in the project and the minigrant contracts that had to be approved by each district and various trustee boards were all on different time lines and required significant staff time from all parties to ensure that tasks and contracts moved forward.

Another challenge to the steering committee was to reconsider the four anticipated target industries in the initial proposal. The realization that project clients were primarily hard to serve and the magnitude of the level of services required to prepare them for training meant that the environmental training track would not benefit this population. Therefore, the steering committee decided to collapse the four industries into three core areas: construction-related trades, machining and precision manufacturing, and automotive technologies and advanced transportation.

Noncollege Partners. As already noted, the construction project area covers over twenty-seven city municipalities and includes state, county, and local governance. The area also includes scores of community-based organizations, a number of economic development agencies, a multitude of local government structures, and various public and private sector entities, all engaged in some level of workforce development and preparation. The challenge was to determine which organizations to work with and what type of relationship would benefit each partner's goals. Staff had to focus on meeting collaborative project goals while navigating the dynamics of working with multiple organizations with different levels of funding, available resources, staff experience, and missions.

The collaborative developed a strategic partnership with the local employment development departments and the Alameda Corridor Jobs Coalition, a public-private sector entity made up of a number of organizations working together to sustain job opportunities for residents of low-income communities. This partnership allowed the collaborative's staff to work more effectively with a number of organizations to do outreach, provide information at job fairs, and receive referred clients for intake, assessment, and referral to the member colleges. Through a variety of partnerships, the collaborative was able to reach out to approximately sixty-nine hundred residents of the region.

Project Challenges: Administration

The most difficult aspect of managing the project was the painstaking and laborious administrative task of keeping track of multiple grants, multiple partner contract relationships, and multiple service contract relationships; tracking data and outcomes dependent on multiple external sources for meeting grant requirements was in itself an enormous task.

Furthermore, the colleges had no additional space, and the grant proposal process was fast-tracked, giving little turnaround time for implementation. Long Beach City College was a member of the Gateway Cities Partnership and had included the partnership in the collaborative project.

Through a leveraging of resources, staff was able to locate at the Gateway Cities office. New job descriptions had to be created, seven staff members were hired, and a number of industry consultants were identified. Working in a merit district and a budget environment at the time that allowed the college to hire approximately 35 percent new faculty over a three-year time period, the administration had to deal with a hiring process that was cumbersome and overburdened.

Finally, the economic development mission of the California Community Colleges required an agile, cost-effective, and flexible response to business and industry needs as mandated by California Government Code §15379.1. The response from most colleges actively engaged in these activities continues to be very impressive, but there are internal barriers at many colleges that can hinder progress.

With eight member colleges, the collaborative had to work under the constraints of multiple internal business practices, all with their own local requirements. Because they had different contract approval process time lines, the contracting process for the minigrants awarded to each college took the most time and required persistent follow-up to encourage colleges to meet performance goals within the project timeline. There were different hiring policies, and contracting and fiscal budgeting had to be done in new ways, thus adding work to already stressed systems and internal staff. The need to work with a variety of business practices also took up much of the time of the collaborative's staff, the lead college, and college members of the consortium.

Project Outcomes

As noted, the initial outcomes for the collaborative were outreach and recruitment to train four hundred people—of which 50 percent were to be welfare recipients—and placement of approximately 50 percent of the total trained into entry-level career-path jobs leading to higher wages. Although some target goals fell under projected numbers, others met and exceeded the initial projections. This section describes targeted project outcomes and explains variances from the initial projections.

Recruitment. Collaborative staff attended Alameda Corridor Transportation Authority (ACTA) "megaorientation" meetings for residents interested in training programs. Outreach through the orientation meetings provided access to training programs in and outside the construction field, personalized services from collaborative career advisers to help clients develop career plans and access workforce preparation services, links to part-time jobs and internships while obtaining training, assistance with and referrals to other support services to alleviate barriers to participation and success, and assistance in beginning appropriate educational and training programs offered by the colleges.

Two recruitment videos were produced for distribution to cable TV, community-based organizations, and local high schools. Six weeks of cable airtime was purchased, targeted to adults ages eighteen to thirty-five earning less than $20,000 per year without a high school diploma. The schedule covered the greater Long Beach region and reached approximately eighty-one thousand households.

All told, presentations were made and direct outreach was done with over 6,900 area residents through megaorientations, community presentations, workshops, and staff outreach at community sites. Of these, the collaborative staff followed up with direct services to 1,785.

Client Demographics. The populations directly served by the collaborative were those who needed job-readiness skills the most: 50 percent were underemployed and sought better employment, 30 percent were leaving welfare, and 20 percent were unemployed. Ethnically, 58 percent were African American, 30 percent were Hispanic, 10 percent were non-Hispanic white, and 2 percent were Asian. Women accounted for 40 percent of those served, men 60 percent.

Job Preparation and Training. Between the efforts of the collaborative and individual college staff, career and basic skills assessments were done for 711 people. By the end of the contract period, 511 people were enrolled at member colleges, 180 had completed training courses, and 351 were continuing. Those who did not enroll at member colleges were referred to other agencies for additional job preparation and life skills support.

Placement. The collaborative established a career path process that addressed job preparation issues and skills, entry-level career path technical and trades training, and preemployment and posttraining support. Because the issue of part-time employment emerged as the number one barrier to enrollment for the average recruit, who was between twenty-five and thirty-seven years old, career advisers also developed part-time employment opportunities to assist the students financially while they were enrolled in college courses. Of the 511 originally enrolled in college courses, 143 (26 percent) were placed into jobs by the end of the contract period. Of these, 66 (13 percent) were welfare recipients. Staff also placed 21 students into paid internships or part-time jobs, and 113 students were referred to "one-stop centers" for permanent placement. In sum, 277 students, or 54 percent, were placed into permanent jobs, part-time work, or internships leading to full employment.

Industry Links. Mutually beneficial relationships were established with business and industry that enabled the collaborative and individual member colleges to link college programs and students to jobs in the region. Face-to-face interview surveys were conducted with fifty-five business owners in manufacturing technology and transportation, and new feedback methods from industry were developed. An updated and enhanced industry database was developed through the industry outreach efforts. A thirty-two-member Machinist Industry Advisory Council was formed to link industry needs to faculty and lead to the development of new curricula. Eight new courses were funded through the minigrant process with the guideline that the courses meet industry needs for placement in entry-level or internship-apprenticeship programs. Participation with the California Transportation Foundation, a nonprofit corporation, connected industry leaders to the automotive technology training models in development with Pep Boys and Midas International. A construction training model was developed in conjunction with the contractors' state license board.

The Model and New Opportunities

Significant outcomes achieved through the collaborative partnership led to new advances at the participating colleges and new opportunities to continue to work together and individually. This included program capacity building at individual colleges; development of faculty and staff expertise; addition of new equipment to update core instructional areas; new and revised college curricula; new college consortium opportunities; enhanced links with industry, employers, and community organizations; new grant-funded opportunities; and increased regional awareness of the ability of community colleges to deliver quality, just-in-time, and valued-added training to the region.

Faculty were able to infuse curricula with updated industry skill sets. Instructional programs in the core industry areas were updated. Curricula were revised and rewritten. In addition, colleges were able to leverage their enhanced services and programs and further develop relationships in the industries served and with regional employers.

Compton College obtained new equipment and enhanced its welding program. Cerritos College was able to obtain a new grant for manufacturing technology, in part through the collaborative's minigrant project accomplishments. Long Beach City College created a new curriculum in its machine tool technology program and was able to obtain a public sector grant serving residents of the region through additional credit-based vocational education. Working in partnership with Gateway Cities Inc., four of the eight colleges came together at the end of the collaborative contract period in a structure similar to the collaborative and developed new multimedia modules in manufacturing technology through a U.S. Department of Labor grant. The modules were designed to upgrade the skills of current workers and in consequence decrease the need for foreign workers.

Economic development and workforce preparation staff at participating colleges developed more effective outreach and recruitment strategies that could be applied to other projects. Los Angeles Trade and Technical College developed additional services to respond to the needs of new students who were on welfare. The collaborative model that linked policy setting to technical assistance, outreach, support services, and new program improvement is currently being applied by Long Beach City College in a number of other projects and has helped the college develop and refine its capacity to deliver programs and services.

Conclusion

A new outreach and customer service mechanism was created to use community college training to help people develop career ladders and get jobs in growing industries in the Gateway Cities region. The economic development goals of the Alameda Corridor Transportation Authority, and all of its funding sources, were greatly expanded through the collaborative project. This project served a large number of clients. Life-changing career-path opportunities were offered to residents of the region who were not directly affected by or attracted to the limited construction jobs available; these people received training and support services through the eight member colleges. The project also met its mandated outcome goals with some modification in projected numbers for placement. It served the residents of the region who lacked workplace skills and had the greatest need for employment. Participants received quality training, obtained first-time certification in many fields, and were able to enter the job market or upgrade skills to get higher-wage jobs.

In sum, the collaborative project met and in some cases exceeded its goals. It brought new resources and funding to economic development efforts. It linked more closely core instruction with current business and industry needs. It demonstrated to individuals and industry in the region the value of a community college education and its cost-effectiveness. It brought together eight colleges into a consortium that leveraged the resources, expertise, and existing strengths of each, enabling them to build capacity for program delivery in response to industry needs. The more lasting benefit to them, however, has been the successful implementation of an innovative community college training model that can be applied in several areas. Through their combined efforts and leveraged resources—and acting seamlessly as one—the colleges made important contributions to the collaborative project and to the mission of economic development and workforce improvement in California.

References

Alameda Corridor Industry & College Collaborative. "Mission Statements." Brochure. Paramount, Calif.: Alameda Corridor Industry & College Collaborative, 1998.

Alameda Corridor Transportation Authority. "Alameda Corridor: A Project of National Significance–Putting California's Economy on the Fast Track to the Future." Los Angeles: Alameda Corridor Transportation Authority, 1999.

California Community Colleges Chancellor's Office, Educational Services and Economic Development Division. "Attachment III, Legislative Intent, Mission, Goals and Strategic Priorities, California Government Code §15379.21." Economic Development Request for Applications: Instructions, Terms and Conditions, 1998–1999. Sacramento: California Community Colleges Chancellor's Office, Educational Services and Economic Development Division, February 1998.

Fogg, N., and Harrington, P. "Growth and Change in the California and Long Beach–Los Angeles Labor Markets." Boston: Center for Labor Market Studies, Northeastern University, 2001.

"Project Paints Picture of Teamwork, Cooperation." *Corridor Chronicles,* 1(4), Spring/Summer 2001.

USC Center for Economic Development, School of Policy, Planning, and Development. "Gateway Cities: A Profile at the Start of the 21st Century." Presented at Gateway Cities Future: Advancing and Sustaining Our Communities for Tomorrow Conference, Long Beach, Calif., February 9, 2001.

LOU ANNE BYNUM is administrative dean of economic development at Long Beach City College, California.

7

This chapter describes the faculty-initiated development of experiential projects with community agencies and businesses as a core requirement for transfer students to become engaged with both their campus and their community.

Learning Into Action: Partnerships Take the Classroom to the Community

Linda P. Woiwod

Skagit Valley College's Learning Into Action program, a loose partnership with a broad range of agencies and businesses, is a catalyst for student learning. It is the result of a strong collaboration between the district's constituencies both on and off campus. A broad array of connections provides the conduit linking students to important business and community initiatives. Business leaders mentor and assist college students in developing curriculum-related skill sets. From the beginning, business and community leaders participated in discussions with faculty and students about the needs and trends they saw developing in their spheres. Internships developed from a combination of curriculum objectives, student goals, and mentor coaching. Business benefits included new customer and social perspectives that emerged as the "teacher" learned from the student. This chapter describes the program, its definition, scope, partner roles, and its application to student learning experiences.

Program Overview

Learning Into Action, a degree requirement for Skagit Valley College transfer students, is an independent project that allows students to apply skills and abilities gained in the classroom setting to their world. Students seeking an associate of arts transfer degree through Skagit Valley College must complete a minimum of one thirty-hour project conducted on or off campus.

Skagit Valley College in Washington State has a history of pioneering innovative and creative educational programs and has a nationally recognized reputation for leading its constituencies in high-quality, cutting-edge offerings. A popular practice among community colleges in the early 1990s was to add experiential education requirements for professional-technical degrees and certificates. Cooperative education was and still is a cornerstone for vocational programs. But few community colleges at that time offered an equivalent experiential degree requirement for students seeking a transfer degree to an academic program. Universities were the entities that housed and espoused civic-mindedness in their students through service learning opportunities, and community colleges consistently offered job-related training programs for vocational students. This college was one of the first community colleges in the Northwest to look at experiential education as a degree requirement for its Associate of Arts, University and College Transfer.

The benefits to the community and to the college are numerous and far-reaching. Learning Into Action students and instructors have become a resource for the leaders in the community, and community leaders are a resource for the development of Skagit Valley College students and staff. Students have reported the benefit to them is learning how to work with a variety of people, how to make a career decision or a college major decision, how to finalize college or career plans, how to be open to options newly discovered, and how to improve interpersonal skills.

Instructors consistently note through Learning Into Action that their students have the immediate benefit of finding their "fit" in the world, have the opportunity for direct experience and analysis of their education, expand their views of the world, and develop a new view of different cultures. Supervisors of Learning Into Action students often say they are impressed with the professional performance and respectful behavior they observe in the students.

Community partners often request that student interns extend their stay past the original internship contract. In addition, often students are employed after the internship has been successfully completed.

Program Concept and Design

Learning Into Action was adopted as a result of a Skagit Valley College faculty-based and faculty-driven cohort that was formed in 1990 to reevaluate the general education requirements for the traditional transfer degree for students in the late twentieth and early twenty-first centuries. Instructors and administrators believed general education to be more complete when students integrate acquired skills and knowledge into action.

Over a three-year time frame, an integrated studies degree was researched, planned, and implemented. Year one of the process was dedicated to conducting research that attempted to include all community constituencies. College researchers sought to discover what should be required of a general education at a community college. Faculty and staff volunteered to interview students, community members, and employees. Committees were called to action to complete specific and focused tasks to answer the question, "What does a graduate of Skagit Valley College need to know?" The constituents responded by expressing the need for more opportunities to apply classroom learning to real life, more offerings that integrated learning experiences between disciplines, and more opportunities to apply reading, writing, and quantitative and communication skills across the curriculum. Year two was devoted to analyzing and synthesizing the researched information. The result was to identify key principles that should be tied to all students' general education. Year three was dedicated to designing the degree requirements and coursework integration that would result in imparting the seven principles to students. Also during the third year, an implementation schedule was devised to make the transition from the former degree requirements to the new degree. Included in the revolutionary degree was a requirement for students to participate in a curriculum-related project that included reflection, analysis, instructor sponsorship, and applied classroom learning. This innovative general education requirement is referred to as Learning Into Action.

Program Approach

"Students who graduate from Skagit Valley College should be able to incorporate their critical thinking skills and a creative process to put into practice specific acquired skills, knowledge, and technologies" (Fredlund and Woiwod, 2000, p. 24). The best way to achieve this goal is to provide a structure by which students—in consultation with faculty mentors and community partners—can plan, design, and complete an independent Learning Into Action project. This educational component is the basis for the partnership among business, community agencies, and Skagit Valley College students. Expectations are clearly outlined for all partners, and assessment materials are developed at the college to ensure consistency in program delivery.

Learning Into Action has thrived as a partner in interdisciplinary offerings and also served as a vehicle for students to explore hands-on career options and community involvement. Learning Into Action projects completed by students are approved in the areas of service learning, travel, internships, research projects, and business ventures. The college commits funds for a full-time administrative staff person whose job is to coordinate the students' projects, ensure accurate tracking and reporting, assist faculty to coordinate service learning experiments, monitor college students who tutor in public schools, conduct site visits with students engaged in off-campus projects, and guarantee training and reflection for the students who are putting their "learning into action."

Partnerships

Finding placements and partners is not easy in the very rural area. Skagit Valley College's service district is described as being "between." It is located in the northwest corner of Washington State between the rugged

Cascade Mountain Range and the Pacific Ocean; between Vancouver, British Columbia, and Seattle, Washington; between two cities bordering on the north and the south whose population numbers tower over the population numbers found in Skagit Valley College's service district; between declining fishing, farming, and forestry industries and burgeoning tourist and retail industries. The college's service district is made up of two campuses, two outlying centers, and one downtown business development center. It is the second oldest college in the state of Washington, first opening its doors in 1926. The year 2002 marks the seventy-fifth anniversary of learning at this rural institution averaging about thirty-four hundred full-time equivalency students per quarter. It is not the biggest community college in the state, nor is it the smallest; again, it is "between."

Of the seven thousand businesses that operate in the community in the college's service district, only four employ more than 150 people. Some 95 percent of the businesses in the area report fewer than 12 employees. National retail chains, such as Wal-Mart, Bon Marché, and J.C. Penney, share advertising space in the one daily newspaper next to cottage businesses and home-based consulting services. Through Learning Into Action projects, Skagit Valley College instructors and students have found these businesses to be some of the best partners in experiential curriculum-based learning. Retail establishments such as Lowe's, Weisfield's Jewelry Stores, Key Bank, Country Wide Insurance, and department stores also provide a wide variety of learning opportunities, ranging from researching the socio-economics of customer traffic patterns to analyzing successful advertising campaigns.

Skagit County Community Action Agency, local human services organizations, and K–12 public schools in the college's service district support art projects, reading tutoring programs, individualized tutoring, and community service projects for the Learning Into Action students. "Breakfast Readers" from Skagit Valley College became mentors not only to elementary school children but also to their parents. A new marketing approach for a local business was developed because a research project revealed the counties' growing ESL population had no way of knowing the services or "deals" that were advertised only in English. Print and radio media were developed by local business to reach out to all new citizens of the community. Gardens were tilled and cared for in the cities of Anacortes and Concrete by students who worked with local nurseries to learn the horticulture secrets that made their agricultural projects successful.

Formal and informal collaborative partnerships have been forged with entities operating in the college's service area communities. Skagit Valley College representatives regularly attend meetings with community groups to make presentations, therefore becoming more visible to stakeholders. Instructors invite agency and business personnel to make presentations to students in classes and to participate in larger group presentations for all students. Finally, Skagit Valley College is a member of the Work Source

Development Consortium with the Department of Social and Health Services, Employment Security, Community Action Agency, Department of Labor and Industries, Upper Skagit Tribes, Swinomish Council, Department of Vocational Rehabilitation, and the local workforce development council. The challenges that arise in working with various groups are met with commitment by college faculty to ensure high-quality performance and student project success.

Close working relationships have been developed with human services and government agencies to make sure that students have a place to do their internships and to link the community's activities and the college's course offerings. Philanthropic associations have funded student projects in gardening with children and transit rider research. These projects help promote business, service, civic-mindedness, and student leadership.

Skagit County Mental Health, Chinook Enterprises, and Skagit Valley College embarked on a program of services for students who are chronic consumers of mental health services. The work done was so successful in its first year that the community action agency donated three-quarters of the funding to continue it for another academic year. The college's multicultural program has made great strides in leadership development and scholarship building thanks to the relationships developed with businesses and agencies led by people of color. Proactive steps taken to invite these influential community members to join in mentoring students resulted in a broader representation on college professional and technical advisory groups.

Several Learning Into Action projects and instructor training programs have been developed with the support of specialized grants. "Kids and Culture" and "Young Speakers Bureau" are projects funded by the American Association of Community Colleges. These collaborative projects match the college's speech and communications department with local emergency-preparedness agencies, members of the international community, and local businesses. Safety issues, such as bicycle safety, are topics researched by middle school students to present to elementary school students. "Kids and Culture" pairs members of the international student and business communities in local elementary schools. These funds also support a women's leadership project that matches women student leaders to journalist and horticultural mentors who serve as partners from the community with the women students. From this partnership a yearbook for a small elementary school developed, as did a community garden in which children and parents engage in the horticulture business locally.

Campus Compact grant funds enabled Skagit Valley College to expand Learning Into Action into a model program for other community colleges. For example, Skagit Valley College students developed a CD that showcases both their successes and the scope of the project. It is currently available on the American Association of Community Colleges Web site, which allows users to download the program files, materials, procedures, and pedagogical landmarks associated with development of a new program. Without these grant funds and local technology leader partners, the production of this portfolio would not have been possible.

The Role of the Faculty

Faculty leaders who designed the general education requirements that created the Learning Into Action program constructed general education learning principles, each with accompanying learning outcomes.

General education is driven by seven principles. Learning Into Action is outlined in Principle VII: "Students who graduate from Skagit Valley College should be able to put into practice a specific body of knowledge or theory. This Principle is accompanied by two expected outcome requirements: (1) Be able to incorporate critical thinking skills and a creative process to plan, design, and complete an independent project. (2) Be able to identify and use specific skills, knowledge, and technologies to carry out a project in experiential learning" (General Education Committee, 1999, p. 12).

Faculty mentors are responsible for submitting the final evaluation of each project. Sixty percent of the faculty have been involved in Learning Into Action projects. The volunteer faculty sponsor judges their connection with the curriculum and their educational integrity and provides an assessment of the student's work and level of adherence to the learning contract. In some situations, community members may be involved in documenting or evaluating projects. Evaluation methods reflect the learning outcomes for the project and are assessed in a wide variety of ways, such as with portfolios, journals, interviews, work logs, demonstration exhibitions, written reports, and papers and oral presentations.

An information package that includes a list of possible projects to attempt, a registration form, a list of faculty mentors and their field of expertise, a learning contract, and project-specific materials from past completed work is made available to students. Educational outcomes identified by faculty for their students include communications, quantitative reasoning, critical thinking, and infusion of cultural pluralism.

Education, physical education, and business administration are the three curriculum areas students most frequently choose for their projects. Education students tutor, survey, instruct, observe, and research; physical education students work with wellness and health issues, coaching, and recreation; business administration students partner with the Internal Revenue Service and sales, business development, and planning entities. Other projects are frequently tied to speech, psychology, biology, chemistry, ethnic studies, art, political science, and journalism.

Externships have been developed for interested faculty to experience their own Learning Into Action project. These are arranged through the Learning Into Action coordinator and provide an opportunity for a minimum ten-hour project. This experience helps instructors explore "the fit." Faculty explore the methods by which the classroom experiences integrate skills into real-life situations. Externship projects also give participants an opportunity to experience or reexperience the broader learning outcomes, which can go undiscovered when teaching for a primary outcome. As with the students, each participant in an externship is required to develop curriculum-related goals and objectives. What appear as learning objectives on written learning contracts are usually cognitive in order to be more easily assessed. A description of specific skills that reflect an upgrading of current skills or a gain of new skills is typical. For example, "The extern will be able to demonstrate three effective techniques for disposing of toxic waste," or "The extern will be able to apply knowledge, skills, and abilities learned in identifying and eliminating the seven most dangerous parasites to the tulip bulb." Like students, the instructors discover that they learn more about themselves, their relation to their environment, and how to apply their learning than just the new skill sets. Student participants are able to make effective career decisions, choose a college major that they are better suited for, focus on a discipline, or find what they do *not* want to do any longer. The computer programmer who discovered she was an excellent instructor and the student who wanted to be a teacher but found he was mismatched with the age group he had chosen are examples of the learning outcomes that may be glossed over because they were not on the list of skill sets to be obtained. Often, these potentially overlooked outcomes provide an unexpected value-added component to the learning experience.

Activities for Implementation

Administration and faculty encourage a variety of potential projects. The range of opportunities includes cooperative education, community service, work study, campus-related activities in the areas of student government and leadership development, work with agencies external to the college to fill a local community need, foreign travel, study abroad, lab-workshop-clinical experience, original research, and exhibits. Students added a young speakers' bureau, a community garden project, and a yearbook publishing project for an elementary school, as well as projects assessing loan patterns in a local bank, evaluating sales contact with customers in a jewelry store, and counting old-growth trees on federal land. The college has a rich history of serving the community through these individual and collaborative contributions by partnering with a vast number of business and community-based organizations, including local school districts and nonprofit organizations. Community needs are addressed through projects that provide thousands of hours of activities. Curriculum and faculty involvement provide the conduit that links students to important community and business initiatives.

Cooperative education staff and professional technical staff work with local agencies to place students from all certificate and degree programs.

The best relationships are between longtime instructors and advisory committees whose members are invited from the community. All professional technical advisory committees include community agencies and local businesses. Professional and technical departments have a long-standing history of partnerships that have been mutually beneficial to specific employers and hundreds of students. For example, discarded computer systems that were donated to the computer repair and instrumentation program were quickly transferred to a local alternative high school. Skagit Valley College students worked with the high school students. Computer components were taken apart and sorted, and the teenagers and their college mentors rebuilt the units. The bonus for the high school students was that they kept the equipment they had built. Similarly, Skagit Valley College truck driving students are the first in line to deliver food to the local food bank. The partnership that was developed with Skagit County's human services department has had a positive impact on the lives of at-risk students and their families.

Assessment

Academic credibility is stressed in all Learning Into Action projects. Rigorous and academically sound assessment is critical in building the authority of the program. The experiential learning component of the Skagit Valley College's general education principles has been designed, promoted, and evaluated by a constituency of faculty. Faculty members work with business partners and students to build and to assess learning contracts. Interpersonal skills, critical thinking, and organizational, occupational, and application skills are examples of the varying components assessed during a project. Employers are asked to rate their experience with the student and the project in the same way.

Assessment of the program during the past nine years has brought about changes and additions in project opportunities, refinement of the initial learning contract expectations, discussions about liability issues when students are required to complete work at off-campus sites, and the role of faculty sponsors. Each year some students see the project as "volunteering" and request formal waivers of the requirement; the irony is that the students who complete their projects are the strongest supporters of the program's pedagogy and outcomes.

Sustaining the Program

The Skagit Valley College administrative team recognizes the need to support students and faculty in building partnerships and projects through the Learning Into Action vehicle. The challenges of partner buy-in, dedicated resources, and student involvement were met early in the process. The program's implementation was supported by the institutional philosophy, resource allocation, and broad but active involvement of faculty, students, student services personnel, and administrators. Funds have been committed to provide an operating budget and full-time support. Work is ongoing to make available in-kind and matching funds for grants that enhance the program. Even in times of uncertain budgets, the institution has kept its promise to the founding principles of general education reform, of which Learning Into Action is a component. Skagit Valley College not only supports the delivery of Learning Into Action as a modality but also supports its review and assessment.

Conclusion

Learning Into Action is a program that benefits nearly all members of the college's service district. Without administrative, faculty, and community support there could be no such partnership in learning. This support comes from planning and assessing together on an ongoing basis. In essence, the partnerships, even those considered already established, are in a constant state of collaboration and communication. The payoff? Learning Into Action builds student leaders who become community leaders who help build other student leaders.

References

Fredlund, E., and Woiwod, L. "Associates in Service Learning." Source notebook and report. Skagit Valley College, Mount Vernon, Wa.: Learning Into Action and Career Services Department, 2000.

General Education Committee. *General Education Guidelines and Implementation: A Source Notebook*. Skagit Valley College. Mount Vernon, Wash.: General Education Committee, 1999. (Originally published 1993)

LINDA P. WOIWOD *is dean of enrollment services at Skagit Valley College, Washington.*

8

A business advisory council provides essential support to workforce development programs, including one that serves individuals with disabilities.

High-Tech Partnering Leads to Learning-Centered Curricula for Individuals with Disabilities

Kathleen S. Hurley

The Center for High-Tech Training for Individuals with Disabilities was established as an independent program at Valencia Community College in 1983 to prepare individuals with severe physical disabilities for challenging high-tech careers. The center's first program offered vocational certification in computer programming. It was developed with technical support from the IBM Corporation, which had created other computer programming courses specifically for severely disabled individuals. Today the center offers two unique vocational programs. Students can receive a certificate in computer-assisted design and drafting (CADD) or personal computer support services. Both programs are twelve hundred clock hours in length and cover basic computer skills, math, Microsoft Office software applications, and professional development, and include advanced technical courses.

This chapter begins with a discussion of the center's formation and the development of the partnership with the business advisory council (BAC). It then describes BAC's role and contribution, addresses the partners' challenges, briefly sketches the center's operation, and concludes with a review of the benefits resulting from the partnership.

The Center's Formation

The development of the program began with a dream that people with disabilities can and will experience vocational success. To this end, business partners became involved; a comprehensive plan for accomplishing the goal was drawn up; a strong, balanced curriculum was developed; regular advisory council meetings were held; and advisory council members became actively involved in areas that interested them. The dream was turned into the reality of a new vocational program at the college thanks to the commitment of leaders in the business community. By acknowledging that one aspect of disability is an individual's state of mind, it became clear that physical limitations could be accommodated in the classroom and in the workplace.

A well-known central Florida disability rights activist contacted Valencia Community College, an institution in Orlando, for a facility and for administrative support. The state of Florida provided a $60,000 grant to pilot the project, and IBM provided a consultant to gain the support of executives at large local companies such as Martin-Marietta, AT&T, Westinghouse, SunBank, Walt Disney World Company, and Red Lobster to establish the first business advisory council (BAC). Today, the center operates in partnership with the college, vocational rehabilitation, workers' compensation, and local companies that employ CADD technicians and personal computer support specialists.

The Development of the Partnership with the Business Advisory Council

Unlike most community college programs, the center is revenue-driven and totally dependent on student tuition and grant funds. The primary source of funds for tuition comes from vocational rehabilitation and workers' compensation. In addition, the center received a five-year grant from the U.S. Department of Education's Projects with Industry Program, which will end in September 2002. Additional support was provided through a five-year grant from the Working Connections program of the American Association of Community Colleges (AACC) and Microsoft. The center was designated as a mentor college under the grant. A large three-year postsecondary disabilities grant from the U.S. Department of Education, Office of Special Education and Rehabilitative Services, provided support from 1997 through 2000. BAC member companies provide additional in-kind support. The center pays students' matriculation fees to Valencia Community College based on the number of clock hours for which they are registered. These fees offset some college costs.

Donations of equipment, other resources, and the involvement of a high-level executive from each company to serve as a member of the center's business advisory council was essential to success. It was believed, correctly, that the BAC's role would be pivotal in developing the program curricula and providing internships and jobs for graduates. The center was able to add a CADD program in September 1987 with a $430,000 federal grant. Significant initial support came from Valencia Community College, with an original goal to make the project financially independent.

The BAC began with the involvement of a few key companies that offered employment in high-tech fields. At one time it had a membership of over 125 individuals. Over time, the membership has changed to reflect changes in the program, the college administration, and the community. Currently, the center's BAC has an active core group of 20 to 25 members. This group works closely with the center's staff and continues to advise on curriculum, mentoring, scholarship development, professional development or soft skills, student evaluations, internships, and job placement.

The BAC is a multidisciplinary professional group. Representatives from a variety of businesses include company presidents, personnel directors, and front-line employees. The BAC also includes representatives from community agencies that support or serve individuals with disabilities. The college is also very proud to have a number of the center's graduates serving on the BAC as representatives from their industries.

The Business Advisory Council's Supportive Role and Contribution

Involvement of the BAC has always been essential to ensure the success of the center and its students. Its members believe in the abilities of people with disabilities. Their commitment grows as they become more involved with the center and its students. The BAC functions in an advisory role on all phases of the program, whereas the college assumes responsibility for personnel and college-related policies. The BAC's founder aggressively pursued key community leaders and businesspeople to provide curriculum design guidance and help in student screening and evaluation. BAC members have participated in the selection of students by reviewing aptitude scores and conducting simulated job interviews. Students with severe physical disabilities who have an interest in and aptitude for computers are always given preference. The classes enroll individuals with a broad range of disabilities including, but not limited to, cerebral palsy, epilepsy, quadriplegia, paraplegia, blindness, deafness, Crohn's disease, chronic obstructive pulmonary disorder (COPD), and amputations. Many kinds of accommodations are provided to ensure the students' success. Some students need mouthsticks to use the computer keyboards. Some need specialized software or keyboard or a trackball mouse. Some have had no work experience. The center's staff works with each student to find his or her best accommodation or adaptation.

One of the primary ways in which the BAC supports the center is through its involvement with the development of the center's curriculum. This involvement in the program's decision-making process helps ensure that the graduates will have the necessary skills to be productive employees from their first day on the job. The curriculum is reviewed on a regular basis to make sure it meets the needs of local industry. The center has a dual curriculum: vocational skills and soft skills or professional development. In

2000, with the advice of the BAC, the center retired the original computer programming curriculum and began a vocational certificate program in personal computer support services. Students are prepared to take industry certification exams in A+ and Network+.

Individual BAC members advise the center on state-of-the-art computer subjects as well as on job-seeking skills. Some give presentations to the classes on interviewing skills, deportment, résumés, and job search techniques. As noted, BAC members are also key to the evaluation of the students. They participate in oral evaluations at several points in the curriculum. They mentor students coming into the program, when they have a high level of anxiety. They assist in the development of scholarship funds. They participate in many functions that are held throughout the year, including an open house, graduation, and an appreciation luncheon.

Regular BAC meetings are held on a monthly basis. All BAC members determine their own level of involvement. They play a vital role with the center's staff and with the students and graduates. One particularly helpful form of assistance is the involvement of BAC members in providing internship slots and placement assistance. Several companies in central Florida, such as Convergys, Walt Disney World Company, and NASA-Kennedy Space Center, have either hired or provided internships for numerous center graduates over many years.

The direct involvement of the BAC ensures that training is responsive to the employment needs of the central Florida business community and to the training needs of individuals with disabilities. The center has been fortunate to have a core group of BAC members who have been involved over many years, and as noted, it has been gratifying when graduates of the center are able to come back as active BAC members.

The Operation of the Center

The center's goals and resources are designed to meet the unique needs of the student constituents.

The Center's Goals. The primary goal for each and every student is employment in a high-tech career path. Placement services are provided to assist students to obtain a living wage and stop needing disability benefits. When this goal is accomplished, successful students often want to give back to their communities. This relationship provides excellent promotional material for the college and the department, allowing the center to serve more of the community. Through the center the college has had the opportunity to go beyond what is required by the Americans with Disabilities Act, expand its vocational offerings, and improve its national and international reputation.

The Center's Resources. At the center the staff believes that the quality and content of instruction exceeds traditional programs, including credit programs. Each student is provided an individual, personalized workstation.

Classroom design facilitates an interactive training approach. Instructors use a combination of lecture and skills practice to teach and reinforce student skills. Early in the students' program they are provided the tools to assess their own individual learning styles. This information is shared with the instructors to ensure that they teach to each individual's preferred style. The center offers state-of-the-art computer facilities; as noted, it was fortunate to receive a Working Connections grant from Microsoft and the AACC for extensive resources. Carl Perkins Vocational Education funds were recently used to upgrade the equipment.

Constituents Served. The center directly serves individuals with severe physical disabilities and employers that hire the center's graduates. Indirectly, the center serves its partners in business, local social service and funding agencies, and the families of students who benefit when they graduate and go to work. The center also serves as an example to the college community of what it means to be learning-centered.

Work-Hardening Experience for Students. Students are provided instruction in a simulated work environment. They attend class full-time and usually are given three to four hours of homework every evening and on weekends. A dress code is enforced, requiring students to wear business attire. The center provides a work-hardening experience for students who have not worked in a long time. Some students must adjust their schedules and build up their strength and stamina to be successful in the real world. They learn their physical capabilities while they acquire vocational and professional skills. Once employed, the companies that hire them often compare their skill levels to those of students who have completed two-year or four-year programs.

Student Successes. The payoff for the students is the start of a new career. One successful graduate of the center's programs found a position at an Orlando architectural firm. He had a severe disability in the form of Crohn's disease and severe arthritis. Crohn's is a gastrointestinal condition. Prior to his disability he had worked as a reprographic technician, making photocopies. After graduation, he was able to obtain an internship at an architectural firm, making $7.00 an hour. Within two years, he was making $25.00 an hour and now is also a member of the center's BAC. Another graduate with a severe orthopedic disability had been employed as an iron-worker before he became disabled. After he graduated from the center, he obtained a position as a CADD technician making $11.50 an hour. Within a year, he was earning $16.00 an hour, with an additional $24.00 an hour in overtime work.

The Partners' Challenges

The primary challenge has been finding ongoing funding to continue the program. Historically, the agencies that support the center through student tuition and federal grants have been its mainstay. As agency budgets are cut and opportunities for federal grants are limited, the center will be unable to sustain its current level of service.

Another challenge is to continue to grow the business advisory council, seeking out new members and ensuring that their efforts are productive and meaningful to them. The focus has always been to meet the continuing needs of students and to seek out and serve individuals who otherwise would not have an opportunity to pursue an education leading to a successful career. Students are given individualized services and instruction, one student at a time.

Although the center has consistently met placement objectives, finding good jobs for graduates is another challenge. The goal is to help each student find the right company and the right job for him or her. Part of the challenge is to educate potential employers about the abilities and skills of individuals with disabilities.

The final challenge is public relations, both inside the college and in the community. The center is constantly striving to keep its mission to educate individuals with disabilities at the forefront, to operate in college processes, and to remain learning-centered. Ongoing college and community support will enable Valencia Community College to maintain its history of success for individuals with disabilities.

Benefits of the Partnership

This education-business partnership benefits everyone: students with disabilities find employment, the college benefits from networking, business finds well-trained employees, and the community benefits by turning tax recipients into tax contributors.

Student Benefits. For students it is a relatively short-term program (usually nine months in length) with a long-term gain. Employed graduates receive good starting salaries and begin a high-tech career path. They are able to support themselves and their families. Through the center, the college has been able to offer short-term, high-quality, intensive training in two high-tech, high-demand job fields. Individuals with severe disabilities are offered the opportunity to take vocational coursework in a mainstream educational setting on a college campus. This arrangement sends a very positive message to the college community about success and the ability to deal with adversity.

College Benefits. The college benefits from the involvement of the business community and the networking opportunities that affords. It also benefits from the center's cutting-edge hardware, software, equipment, and accommodations for individuals with disabilities. The focus on individuals with severe disabilities inspires others to strive and grow.

Business and Community Benefits. The community benefits from a decrease in the number of individuals who are dependent on federal, state, and local programs. Businesspeople learn about disability, courage, and the will to succeed, in addition to finding a good source of well-trained employees. BAC members believe that there is a clear return on their investment of time and passion. One BAC member has written the following:

The return is:

- *Not just*—being a major part of the incredible growth and accomplishment of students
- *Not just*—helping students change from "field laborer" mentality to professional orientation
- *Not just*—seeing students placed with local and international corporations
- *Not just*—hiring an intern and finding that person to be your highest achiever

The return for the Valencia Center for High-Tech Training BAC is knowing that the time invested in the program has a greater sense of reward and accomplishment by the hour than the time invested in any other available academic support opportunity. This belief is a constant from year to year, resulting from the BAC-Center structure, [and] is not changed as members or staff join or leave. [Wilkinson and Hurley, 2001]

Conclusion

The Center for High-Tech Training for Individuals with Disabilities offers a unique combination of design, concepts, and curriculum to meet the needs of the local business community. It offers an incredible set of skills and expertise in the form of its staff and students. It offers hope for those courageous individuals who desire to work; it offers results in the form of an entry-level job in a field that historically has offered immense opportunity. It integrates the development of vocational and professional skills with job placement assistance. It brings together the support of the business community with that of social service agencies.

The center strives to provide the best learning environment possible and is committed to supporting the instructors, providing cutting-edge equipment, and offering professional development. The successful student outcomes are the result of teamwork, professionalism, persistence, and concern. It is a program that is truly learning-centered.

Reference

Wilkinson, H., and Hurley, K. "The CADD Connection: Walt Disney World Company and the Center for High-Tech Training for Individuals with Disabilities." Paper presented at the Association of Rehabilitation Providers in Computer Technology (ARPCT) annual conference, Vancouver, B.C., May 24, 2001.

KATHLEEN S. HURLEY *is director of the Center for High-Tech Training for Individuals with Disabilities, Valencia Community College, Florida.*

9

The elements necessary for establishing a successful partnership with business and the community and the types of challenges faced by these relationships are drawn from the readings as general observations.

Concluding Observations on Successful Partnerships

Mary S. Spangler

Clearly one of the strengths of community colleges is their flexibility in connecting to their various and multiple communities in various and multiple ways. Nowhere else, perhaps, is this reality more visible or meaningful than in those partnerships that are based on the concept of "community" in the community college. Partnerships are increasingly becoming an integral strategic element in college operations and illustrate one way in which colleges, businesses, and the community can be bound together for mutual benefit. They are campus-based programs that do not rely on statewide mandates or funding, although such funding is sometimes sought and received. There is no single way to make the connection. The chapters in this volume demonstrate the range, depth, ingenuity, flexibility, and accessibility of just a handful of successful partnerships in place across the country.

Why Projects Succeed

There is no one model or process to follow in establishing a successful partnership between a community college and the general community. Different numbers of partners may be involved. Several examples included here involve one college with several partners, whereas one describes a relationship between one college and one other entity. Partnerships can spring from a unique onetime opportunity or form as a result of a significant, ongoing need. They are not limited by geographic location, economic status, or demographic characteristics. They may directly involve faculty and students or be driven by administrative goals. Nevertheless, all of the partnerships have some common elements. All offer economic benefit to the partners. All require the involvement and commitment of the institution's leadership. All directly benefit students.

It is clear from the chapters in this volume that these projects moved from concept to reality because of the flexibility that community colleges, in general, are able to exercise if and when they choose to do so. First, their core missions are flexible. The emphasis now placed on connection to community has ushered in a new era in developing relationships with external constituencies. In addition, the colleges' physical closeness to the students and communities they serve makes them more approachable and more attractive to potential partners than most four-year institutions. Although regulations, policies, and statutes limit the organizations from within and without, community colleges pride themselves on being user-focused and service-oriented. Motivated by this will to serve, leaders have found ways through the bureaucratic morass that they inevitably encounter during the development and implementation stages of any new undertaking.

As illustrated by the partnerships, an equally important but less recognized reason for success is that community colleges are becoming more willing than they used to be to engage in entrepreneurial activities. Although it is true that the educational enterprise has not been traditionally well prepared to identify and respond to business opportunities, many college leaders have recognized that they need to consider this avenue in response to external realities. For example, attention to vocational programs and workforce needs has increased as relationships with employers and advisory councils have proliferated in response to state and federal actions. Thus, colleges' access to and understanding of entrepreneurial opportunities have been stimulated. At the same time, the community college's ability to rely on state and local funding has been challenged. Responsive institutions now recognize the need to develop alternative funding sources. To manage, many colleges are becoming adept at functioning in a client-driven, business-oriented environment.

Unlike the traditional academic environment where programs often persist despite poor outcomes, lack of student participation, or failure to remain current, business and community partnerships survive only as long as they are effective, efficient, productive, profitable, and outcome-oriented for the partner. Thus the relationship must serve the employer, community, and business, if it is to survive. Community colleges have been able to capture that element in the partnership and exploit it for their students. There is, therefore, a continuing benefit for all those involved in the relationship. Often, benefits or positive outcomes extend beyond what was originally intended or anticipated when the partnership was created. Unplanned outcomes can be available for the college, the partner, students, and the community at large. For the colleges, those benefits include an increased ability and willingness to take on new entrepreneurial commitments.

Success is usually not decided by the singular strengths of an individual partner but rather by a divergent set of skills and circumstances.

Certainly, among the most significant skills providing the sustaining force are vision, creativity, persistence, determination, and tolerance for prudent risk-taking. Although just plain luck can help create the opportunity needed to connect, trust must be established and nurtured between the partners if the relationship is to develop and thrive.

Some Challenges

Focusing on ensuring that the essential elements of success are in place will not guarantee that partnerships develop or flourish. It is to be expected that throughout the relationship there will be inevitable challenges. The best planning will not identify all the potential problems. Many of those problems are situational, the result of the unique qualities of the specific relationship. However, there are obvious ones that cannot be avoided.

Chief among the obvious challenges is the necessity to identify each other's needs and expectations clearly. Openly sharing goals and objectives is essential. When obstacles are encountered along the way, it is wise to return to the initial goals and objectives and determine whether they have changed for any one of the partners. If so, those goals need to be reframed, or the relationship will be unlikely to move forward.

The challenge of involving the private business community with the bureaucracy of the public community college is often enough to end a potential partnership. The private organization's experience with making prompt business decisions and acting on them is sure to be tested when working with a heavily regulated public agency. The need for multiple, convoluted approval processes often appears unnecessary and inefficient to the business partner. Statutory regulations often require as much time on the part of the community college partner to explain as to adhere to for the business partner. Although they make good sense to the public agency, they are confounding and maddening for the private entity. The ultimate frustration for the community partner is the necessity for the community college partner to consult with and develop the support of multiple constituencies—faculty, staff, and students—before it can make a substantive commitment.

A business partner may not be prepared for the institution's reluctance to change from traditional ways of delivering instruction to engage in innovative delivery of curriculum and services. Making this paradigm shift requires diplomacy, tact, and an understanding of the faculty's expertise and how they perceive themselves. An effective college leader can provide the partner with invaluable assistance and also help bring the faculty to accept what they might otherwise oppose.

Not to be overlooked is the necessity for integrating potentially differing organizational missions and administrative styles. When two or more entities intend to enter into a collaborative relationship, especially one that needs to be negotiated, the "fit" between the missions of the partnering entities has to be feasible. Assuming it is, the personal connection between the leading players has to be positive, too. Otherwise, the tension and delays will frustrate the most patient partners and create new tensions and frustrations. As a result, expectations and objectives will not be realized, and the critical element of trust will be missing and likely lead to failure for the partnership.

Another obstacle to overcome is the decision about the governance or control of the facility, project, or program. Issues to be resolved include hiring faculty and staff, determining salary and compensation, and agreeing on oversight of facilities. Generally, private partners assume that these issues can be resolved according to their expectations and are not prepared to confront contractual agreements that limit their options. Tenure, curriculum control, and management of college-owned facilities are sure to test the commitment of most potential partners. Time is well spent helping community partners to understand the restrictions imposed on institutions and find ways to accomplish their objectives.

A future topic for consideration would be the new kind of leadership and management skills necessary for bringing complex partnerships to fruition. It has also been suggested that more active involvement of the faculty and students in developing and maintaining partnerships would be a positive expansion of what is now apparently a largely administrative activity.

Partnerships reflect the flexibility, complexity, sophistication, vision, and persistence with which community colleges are establishing connections and pursuing their core missions despite many challenges. Certainly, for the community college leader considering a partnership with business or the community, it is critical to be a problem solver at heart. The individual must literally enjoy the challenge of working through known and unknown obstacles. Refusing to be overwhelmed or discouraged by setbacks is another essential characteristic. These endeavors are not for the faint of heart, but they are worth the effort when there is benefit to students. As these chapters have shown, effective and successful partnerships are the catalyst to raise a college's level of interdependence and connection with business and the community.

MARY S. SPANGLER is president of Los Angeles City College, California.

10

An annotated bibliography of successful partnerships in community colleges is provided, including explanations of how the partnerships developed, discussions of current collaborations, reviews of statewide reports, samples of handbooks, and an analysis of one statewide effort to conduct an outcome measurement of its programs.

Sources and Information: Partnerships with Business and the Community

Fred Piegonski

During the last decade, community colleges across the United States have increasingly seen the importance of developing entrepreneurial relationships with private industry. As the chapters in this volume show, these relationships have developed in various ways.

This chapter reviews some of the current ERIC literature on community colleges and their relationships with business and industry. The focus for this bibliography is material that sheds light on how these collaborations began and prospered. Included are articles, reports, and books that chronicle current partnerships, focus on the process that led up to the partnerships, outline statewide recommendations, discuss tech prep handbooks, and show how one state measured the effectiveness of its economic development programs.

ERIC documents (listings with "ED" numbers) may be read on microfiche at approximately nine hundred libraries throughout the world. Most documents may also be ordered on microfiche or paper copy from the ERIC Document Reproduction Service (EDRS) at (800) 443–ERIC. For a list of libraries housing ERIC microfiche documents, contact the ERIC Clearinghouse for Community Colleges at (800) 832–8256 or visit ericcc@ucla.edu.

Journal articles may be acquired through libraries, from the journal publisher, or for a fee from the article reproduction vendor Ingenta; call (617) 395–4046 or (800) 296–2221 or e-mail help@ingenta.com. See also http://www.ingenta.com.

NEW DIRECTIONS FOR COMMUNITY COLLEGES, no. 119, Fall 2002 © Wiley Periodicals, Inc.

The Process Leading Up to Partnerships

Several publications provide information on how to develop community college–business partnerships.

Building a Regional Bridge from Education to Careers in Partnership with Business, Industry, Government, and Education: A Regional Planning Process Model for K–14 Career Education with Employer Linkages. Sacramento: California Community Colleges, 1992. (ED 347 386)

The Antelope Valley (California) Bridge from Education to Careers is a regional plan for developing a local program of career education to prepare all students from kindergarten through community college for careers. Recommendations for a model process are based on the Antelope Valley experience. There are twenty-six steps to building a regional bridge from education to careers: identify core leadership; designate a team leader; identify potential organizations; plan time lines; conduct the first meeting; identify employer concerns; identify planning issues; build cooperation between business and education; identify a leadership group; review existing career development materials; develop a mission statement; obtain feedback about mission statement; identify subcommittees; identify tasks; conduct both committee and subcommittee meetings in same time block; conduct meetings with chairs; prepare committee reports; identify process to achieve mission; identify employer liaisons; design a visual representation of process; develop documents for committee review; route draft documents for review; develop implementation plan; prepare final document; implement plan; and coordinate implementation. The following items are included in this booklet: twelve tips for the building committee, twenty-four ideas for building employer liaisons, information on the Antelope Valley career guide, and steering committee members.

Cantor, J. A. *Cooperative Apprenticeships: A School-to-Work Handbook.* Lancaster, Pa.: Technomic, 1997. (ED 405 471)

Explains the process of designing, developing, and implementing a cooperative apprenticeship, a form of structured workplace training in which an employer, employer group, union, or other community-based organization joins forces with a vocational-technical school or a community college to provide formal instruction that includes structured work-based experience. The following topics are among those discussed in the book's first nine chapters: characteristics of cooperative apprenticeship; steps in building school-to-work collaboratives; needs assessment and marketing; a school-to-work concept for preapprenticeship and youth apprenticeship programs; design and development of apprenticeship programs; recruitment, screening, and selection of apprentices and employers; related classroom education and educational support; and apprentice testing, evaluation, and certification. Listed in Chapter Ten are associations, sources of government assistance, newsletters, periodicals, and books likely to be useful to individuals involved in developing cooperative apprenticeship programs. The book contains forty-six tables and eighty-one end-of-chapter references. Appended are U.S. Department of Labor Standards for apprentice program registration and lists of the following: apprenticeable occupations, Bureau of Apprenticeship and Training state offices and state apprenticeship councils, labor commissioners' and regional directors' state-level contacts, and Bureau of Apprenticeship and Training regional offices.

Hensley, O. D., and others (eds.). *The Tech Prep Handbook: Essential Documents to Promote Effective Tech Prep Policies and Practices.* Austin: Texas Higher Education Coordinating Board, 1996. (ED 402 453)

Developed during a project to document and analyze the tech prep initiative in Texas, this handbook contains exemplary documents associated with the model programs in the state. This second edition organizes documents in sections that correspond to the major impact sectors identified during the research project: (1) tech prep consortia; (2) colleges and universities; (3) disciplinary bodies; (4) government; and (5) industry and business. Document types include consortia agreements, competency lists, courses of study, flowcharts, program descriptions, summaries of legislation, articulation guides, and publicity flyers. A glossary defines ninety-one terms.

Hensley, O. D., and others (eds.). *The Tech Prep Handbook: Performance Assessment.* Austin: Texas Higher Education Coordinating Board, 1997. (ED 408 469)

This handbook for tech prep practitioners in Texas consists of looseleaf documents from the performance assessment areas currently available to tech prep practitioners. The first part of the handbook includes ten sample assessment documents selected from over nine hundred performance assessments based on a quantitative rating system. The documents, which are intended as guides for teachers developing their own assessment instruments and processes, are as follows: "Status Report May 1997: Summary of Statewide Data on Programs and Baseline Student Characteristics," "1994–95 Tech Prep Graduate Survey," "Assessment of Business and Industry Needs for Guadalupe County," "Intergenerational Professions Information Packet for Intergenerational Professions for Tech Prep," "Award-Winning Lesson Plans for Integrating Workplace Skills into the Classroom," "Competency-Outcomes for Tech Prep Programs and Crosswalks to SCANS [Secretary's Commission on Achieving Necessary Skills] Skills," "Competency Profile CAGR 1302 Microcomputer Operating Systems," "Real World Portfolios," "The Master Plan for Career and Technical Education," and "State Occupational Information Coordinating Committee Activities for 1995." The remainder of the document details the findings of the 1997 survey of nineteen of Texas's twenty-five tech prep consortia. Appended are the student outcomes questionnaire and the geographic representation of responses to the questionnaire.

Illinois Tech Prep Planning Strategies. Springfield: Illinois State Board of Education, Department of Adult, Vocational, and Technical Education, 1991. (ED 345 021)

This tech prep planning handbook is based on the research conducted at the Office of Community College Research and Leadership, University of Illinois at Urbana-Champaign. The study involved information-gathering procedures at each of the seventeen tech prep pilot sites about their planning activities. Seven sections are included: (1) tech prep in Illinois; (2) applying the tech prep planning process; (3) involving key groups in planning tech prep; (4) developing the components of tech prep—local policies, staff development, articulated curriculum, curriculum development, written agreements, guidance and counseling, marketing, and business-industry collaboration; (5) putting tech prep into action; (6) evaluating the tech prep plan; and (7) four appendixes: contributors, words of advice, 1990–91 tech prep initiatives' profiles, and suggested resources (of which there are fifteen).

Oregon Tech Prep–Associate Degree Program: Developing a High Performance Workforce. Salem: Oregon State Department of Education, 1992. (ED 346 907)

Issued jointly by Oregon's Superintendent of Public Instruction and the Commissioner of Community Colleges, this policy statement is aimed at implementing the Oregon Tech Prep–Associate Degree Program, a new applied academics curricular structure. The paper begins with a summary of Oregon's school reform efforts, an open letter to the leaders of Oregon high schools and community colleges, a statement of the problem of addressing the educational and curricular needs of students who are unlikely to complete a baccalaureate, and four benchmarks concerning the education and job training of high school students into the year 2010. Next, an introduction describes the need for this degree program, emphasizing the ways in which such a program removes barriers to educational excellence. After providing a definition of the tech prep–associate degree program, the paper proposes that the following steps be taken to initiate Oregon's program: (1) develop a structured and substance-rich applied academics curriculum; (2) develop and implement high standards, achievement expectations, and assessment policies; (3) develop learning and guidance strategies; (4) provide teacher and counselor preservice and in-service programs; (5) develop the curriculum through collaboration between high school and college faculty, regional professional technical education coordinators, education service districts, and employer representatives; (6) develop strategies aimed at changing student and public attitudes about professional technical training; and (7) develop community college "bridge" programs to prepare adult students to move into this new program. For each of the seven proposed steps, a number of more specific activities are explored. Notes and references are also included.

Perfumo-Kreiss, P., and Harrison, L. *Economic Development at the Grass Roots: A Guide for Creating Partnerships Between Main Street Programs and California Community Colleges.* Sacramento: California Community Colleges, Office of the Chancellor, 1991. (ED 350 016)

The California Main Street program provides technical assistance to rural communities facing rapid growth and downtown decay, serving as a vehicle for local stimulation and revitalization of downtown area businesses. This five-part handbook presents strategies for creating partnerships between California's Main Street programs and the state's community colleges. Following an introduction, which details the development and structure of both this new program and the California community colleges, "The Mutual Benefits of Cooperation" discusses advantages and constraints of the partnership for both entities. Next, "Defining the Relationship" reviews the roles and responsibilities of participants and provides examples of college departments and the assistance they might provide in cooperative arrangements. In "Case Studies," profiles and contact information are presented for the Auburn Main Street–Sierra College partnership, through which Sierra College provided a student intern to Main Street, and Main Street supported Sierra College's Small Business Development Center; the Quincy Main Street–Feather River College partnership, which has involved Main Street providing advice to Feather River College on curriculum development, and the two entities working together to develop a summer arts and entertainment series and a student community service program; and the Fort Bragg Main Street–College of the Redwoods partnership, which has involved college students in the design and analysis of a Main Street consumer survey and joint fundraising. The handbook concludes with a chapter that provides advice on how to initiate a contract and develop the relationship. The chapter focuses on fostering communication and trust. Appendixes provide directories of Main Street communities, community colleges, and small business development centers in the state.

Vivelo, F. R. "The Nature and Operation of Training Institutes: A Generic Marketing Plan for Community Colleges." *Community Services Catalyst,* Winter 1991, *21*(1), 13–21.

Discusses marketing problems and opportunities associated with satisfying demand, product-consumer match, support services, personnel, and personal involvement. Identifies overall marketing and business-financial goals and related objectives. Covers action plans, performance evaluations, curriculum design, advisory committee participation and input, partnerships with prospective employers, community participation, and administrator and instructor roles.

Partnerships of Current Interest to Community Colleges

The following entries provide a glimpse of some recent partnerships that are unusual or of compelling interest to community college professionals.

Commission on the Future of Howard Community College, Progress Report 2000. Columbia, Md.: Howard Community College, Office of Planning and Evaluation, 2000. (ED 446 789)

Presents the Commission on the Future of (Maryland's) Howard Community College's progress report for 2000. The report's third section, "Collaboration with Business and Industry," looks at strategic process priorities, such as establishing a strategy to create and enhance partnership opportunities, becoming more proactive than reactive in responding to the needs of the community, establishing Howard Community College as an important resource in the county, providing a variety of business and professional exchanges and opportunities, and building relationships and partnerships. Section Four, "Economics and Workforce Development," outlines strategic process, tactical recommendations, and discusses other issues and ideas, including Howard's need to expand its use of e-commerce tools. Section Five, "Preparing Students as Global Citizens," discusses participating with community groups in developing global competencies and implementing technology and global initiatives.

Eller, R., Martinez, R., Pace, C., Pavel, M., and Barnett, L. *Rural Community College Initiative IV: Capacity for Leading Institutional and Community Change.* AACC Project Brief. Annapolis Junction, Md.: Community College Press, 1999. (ED 432 332)

Reports on the Ford Foundation's establishment of the Rural Community College Initiative for selected institutions in economically distressed areas of the Southeast, the deep South, the Southwest, Appalachia, and Indian reservations in the West. The initiative program challenges community colleges to become catalysts for change by working toward two goals: expanding access to higher education and fostering regional economic development. This brief examines the experiences of the nine pilot colleges and their efforts to acquire the capacities for change, and identifies implications for other institutions facing similar challenges. It suggests that an institution's capacity to meet these two goals requires attention to institutional cultures, leadership style, and organizational infrastructure. In strengthening these areas, community colleges can improve their effectiveness in building human resources and social capacities for survival and success in a changing world. Colleges must look seriously at new roles, partnerships, and marketing, as well as value systems that include team-building strategies, risk taking, and openness to expanded access, economic development, and local cultures. Contains twelve references.

Folsom, B. "The Role of Community Colleges in the Emerging Domestic and Global Economy." *Catalyst,* Summer 1999, *28*(2), 13–17.

Examines the role of community colleges in the middle class's increased wages, the implementation of the School to Work Act, the impact of corporate partnerships, and the influence of global competition on economic factors. Closes with a view of the central role that community colleges will play in the economic future of the country. Contains eighteen references.

Garrett, R. L., and Parker, W. A. "A Regional Economic Development Partnership for Community-Based Programming." Paper presented at the Team Building for Quality Conference of the National Initiative for Leadership and Institutional Effectiveness, Greensboro, N.C., October 14–17, 1995. (ED 393 523)

Florence-Darlington Technical College in Florence, South Carolina, has implemented the Academy for Community College Leadership Advancement, Innovation, and Modeling (ACCLAIM), a community-based programming model for developing a regional economic development strategic plan. The ACCLAIM model was designed to assist the 114 community colleges in North Carolina, South Carolina, Virginia, and Maryland in expanding their mission and leadership roles to put greater emphasis on community-based programming. The model is composed of fifteen tasks providing a systematic approach to solving community issues and is designed to result in the identification and resolution of major issues, the creation of cooperative and unified efforts, the acceptance of high community expectations among community members, and the emergence of new leaders. As a result of implementing the ACCLAIM model, this college established community-based training institutes and regional economic development partnerships. Problems encountered in implementing the process included a lack of communication and skepticism among participants. Appendixes provide a list of significant employers, information on the ACCLAIM model, and time lines and organizational charts related to college initiatives. This grant-based program is no longer in existence.

Patt, B. E. "California Schools Develop Joint Faculty Journalism Project." *Community College Journalist,* 1995, *23*(1–4), 16–19, 36–37.

Describes the Joint Faculty Journalism Project, undertaken in 1994–95 by California's community colleges and universities, to develop methods for increasing alliances with journalists. Discusses project objectives and resulting recommendations related to increasing student recruitment and success. Reviews positive project outcomes and a local application of recommendations in the Sacramento area. This program's activities were completed in 1995.

Sink, D. W. Jr., and Jackson, K. L. "Bridging the Digital Divide: A Collaborative Approach." *Community College Journal,* Oct.-Nov. 2000, *71*(2), 38–41.

Twelve rural North Carolina colleges facing decisions about campus technology investments chose to form a technology alliance to share information, identify critical needs, rethink budget development and funding formulas at local and state levels, leverage resources, and cooperate in new ventures. Includes recommendations for other colleges trying to leverage technology resources.

Statewide Recommendations

The following works provide proscriptive reports from California and Kentucky. The first focuses exclusively on California's community colleges and economic development issues, and the second chronicles recommendations for Kentucky's community colleges, including economic development issues.

Callahan, L., and others. "Golden State, Golden Opportunity: Vocational Education and Economic Development in California Community Colleges." Issue Paper. Sacramento: Chief Executive Officers of the California Community Colleges, Mar. 1990. (ED 326 292)

Intended as the beginning of an ongoing review of the California Community Colleges' vocational education programs, academic certificate and degree programs, and short-term job skills and retraining programs, this paper sets out to define economic development and clarify its role in the community college context; develop a consensus among chief executive officers on the definition and role of economic development; raise the consciousness of community college leaders at the state and local levels about the need for and potential of economic development activities; and develop specific recommendations to improve vocational education and economic development programs in the state's colleges. The paper is divided into six main sections. Following a brief introduction, Section Two presents a glossary of terms related to the concepts of vocational education and economic development. Section Three discusses the problems faced by community colleges in providing effective vocational training in light of the growing emphasis on transfer education. Section Four discusses the implications of Assembly Bill 1725 and the final report of the Joint Legislative Committee on Vocational Education. Section Five presents a proposed policy statement for California's colleges, examining institutional mission as it relates to economic development. Section Six offers a set of recommendations from the chief executive officers of the state's colleges to the board of governors, the chancellor's office, and the district offices. A literature review, the board of governors' vocational education and employment training policy, and a list of vocational education courses at colleges throughout California are appended.

Miller, K., and others (eds.). *Community Colleges: Pathway to Kentucky's Future. Futures Commission Report* (2nd ed.). Lexington: Kentucky University Community College System, 1996. (ED 391 551)

In 1989, the Commission on the Future of the University of Kentucky Community College System issued recommendations for improving the colleges' role, effectiveness, and potential. This report assesses the progress made as of 1995 with respect to these recommendations in several areas, including postsecondary technical education and economic and workforce development. For each issue, the report provides a summary of the current status as well as commission recommendations and the rationale behind the recommendations. Important recommendations for 1995 include to develop more collaborative processes and partnerships that result in joint ventures with the Kentucky TECH System for community development; increase responses to business and industry needs with technical degree programs, job specific training and retraining, and services; and strengthen the effectiveness of the local advisory boards.

Measuring Outcomes

Once you put an economic development program in place, how do you measure its success to justify continued funding? The following article describes how the state of California objectively measured the outcomes of its community college economic development programs.

Kirschenmann, S., and Lane, T. "Measuring Outcomes of Community College Economic Development Programs." *Community College Journal,* June–July 2001, 71(6), 14–17.

In 1998, California's state legislature imposed an outcome measurement requirement on the Economic Development Program of the California Community Colleges. Through discussion with state government policy and fiscal analysts, it became clear that desirable characteristics of the outcome evaluation would include collection of defensible data, estimation of programmatic benefit–cost ratio, and measurement of the growth and profitability of businesses served. Thus, evaluating economic development program outcomes required an assessment of business success associated with the programs. To accomplish this task, employers receiving benefits throughout the state were identified with their federal employer identification numbers. The state calculated annual wages paid and average monthly employment for both the employers served through economic development and comparison company samples. This was done for three years. The state tax board records helped determine the profitability of both samples. Outcomes then consisted of benefit-cost ratios for all community college economic development programs and a fiscal rate of return—defined as the net present value of state tax revenues over the next ten years resulting from community college economic development programs. For 1998–99, estimated economic development benefits were $262 million. Total budgeted costs were $33 million, with a benefit cost ratio of 7.9. The fiscal return on investment was $1.42, meaning that California will collect $1.42 in taxes over the next ten years for every dollar it spent on economic development programs in 1997–98. This outcomes process is now conducted annually.

Additional Sources

Becherer, J. J., and Becherer, J. H. "Nest for Dreams, Backdrops for Visions: Making a Difference with Students." In M. M. Culp and S. R. Helfgot (eds.), *Life at the Edge of the Wave.* Washington, D.C.: National Association of Student Personnel Administrators, 1998.

Bragg, D. D., and others. *Tech Prep–School-to-Work Partnerships: More Trends and Challenges.* Berkeley: National Center for Research in Vocational Education, University of California at Berkeley, 1997.

Dornsife, C. "The Postsecondary Partner." In E. N. Andrew and others (eds.), *Lessons Learned: Five Years in the Urban Schools Network.* Berkeley: National Center for Research in Vocational Education, University of California at Berkeley, 1997.

Kussrow, P. G. *Why Community Colleges Need Organizational Partnership.* Unpublished report, 1995. (ED 386 230)

Marrow, A. J., and McLaughlin, J. *Community Collaboration: A Creative Partnership with Catonsville Community College.* Paper presented at Leadership 2000 Seventh Annual International Conference of the League for Innovation in the Community College and the Community College Leadership Program, San Francisco, July 1995. (ED 396 796)

Orr, M. T. "Integrating Secondary Schools and Community Colleges Through School-to-Work Transition and Educational Reform." *Journal of Vocational Education Research,* 1998, 23(1), 93–111.

Tafel, J., and Eberthart, N. *Statewide School-College (K–16) Partnerships to Improve Student Performance.* Denver, Colo.: State Higher Education Executive Officers, 1999.

Terrell, M., and Watson, L. "Collaborative Partnerships for a Diverse Campus Community." *Journal of College Student Development,* 1996, 37, 249–253.

FRED PIEGONSKI *is executive assistant to the president at Los Angeles City College, California.*

INDEX

ACCLAIM (Academy for Community College Leadership Advancement, Innovation, and Modeling) model, 87

Alameda Corridor Industry & College Collaborative: challenges of, 51–54; conclusions about, 57; description of, 47–48; mission of, 48; outcomes for, 54–56; participants of, 49–51; structure of, 48

Allen, J. P., 2, 36

Annotated bibliography, 81–90

Antelope Valley (California) Bridge from Education to Careers, 82

Apprenticeships, cooperative: and Center for Manufacturing Excellence, 13–19; in electrical construction, 2–3, 31–36; literature on, 82–83; in machine technology, 3, 37–46

Asnuntuck Community College's machine technology program: benefits from, 44–45; conclusions on, 45–46; curriculum for, 42–43; development of, 3, 38–42; internships in, 41; purpose of, 38; and student outcomes, 43–44

Autonomy and partnering, 11

Barnett, L., 86

Belcher, A., 13

Bibliography, annotated, 81–90

Brouillette, L., 13

Buettner, D. L., 2, 12

Burd, S., 13

Business advisory council's role in a partnership, 70–72

Bynum, L. A., 3, 58

California, workforce improvement in, 3. See also Alameda Corridor Industry & College Collaborative

California community colleges: Joint Faculty Journalism Project at, 87; Long Beach City College, 3, 47–57; Los Angeles City College, 2, 4, 21–29; recommendations for, 88

California Main Street program, 85

Callahan, L., 88

Cantor, J. A., 82

Carl Sandburg College, partnership development process at, 2, 13–19

Center for High-Tech Training for Individuals with Disabilities, 3, 69–75

Center for Manufacturing Excellence (CME), 2, 13–19

CEOs, commitment of, 10

Crist, D. G., 14, 18

Curriculum: for electrical construction technology degree, 34–35; for machine technology program, 42–43

Degree programs: in electrical construction technology, 2–3, 31–36; in machine technology, 3, 37–46

Disabilities, training center for students with: benefits from, 74–75; business advisory council's role in, 70–72; challenges for, 73–74; formation of, 3, 69–70; operation of, 72–73

Economic opportunity, as seed of partnership, 7

Electrical construction technology degree program, 2–3, 31–36

Eller, R., 86

Externships, 65

Faculty's role in Learning Into Action program, 64–65

Flexibility in partnerships, 10–11, 78

Fogg, N., 50

Folsom, B., 87

Fredlund, E., 61

Garrett, R. L., 87

Goals, shared, 6

Golf facility, development of on-campus, 22–28

Greenleaf, R. K., 11

Gulluni, F., 3, 46

Harrington, P., 50

Harrison, L., 85

Hensley, O. D., 83

Hurley, K. S., 3, 75

Back Issue/Subscription Order Form

Copy or detach and send to:

Jossey-Bass, A Wiley Company, 989 Market Street, San Francisco CA 94103-1741

Call or fax toll-free: Phone 888-378-2537 6AM-5PM PST; Fax 888-481-2665

Back issues: Please send me the following issues at $28 each.

(Important: please include series initials and issue number, such as CC114)

1. CC _____

_____

_____

$ _____ Total for single issues

$ _____ SHIPPING CHARGES: SURFACE

	Domestic	Canadian
First Item	$5.00	$6.00
Each Add'l Item	$3.00	$1.50

For next-day and second-day delivery rates, call the number listed above.

Subscriptions: Please ❑ start ❑ renew my subscription to *New Directions for Community Colleges* for the year 2____ at the following rate:

U.S.	❑ Individual $66	❑ Institutional $135
Canada	❑ Individual $66	❑ Institutional $175
All Others	❑ Individual $90	❑ Institutional $209

$ _____ Total single issues and subscriptions (Add appropriate sales tax for your state for single issue orders. No sales tax for U.S. subscriptions. Canadian residents, add GST for subscriptions and single issues.)

Federal Tax ID 135593032   GST 89102 8052

❑ **Payment enclosed** (U.S. check or money order only)

❑ **VISA, MC, AmEx, Discover Card #** _____ Exp. date_____

Signature _____ Day phone _____

❑ **Bill me** (U.S. institutional orders only. Purchase order required)

Purchase order #_____

Name _____

Address _____

Phone_____ E-mail _____

For more information about Jossey-Bass, visit our Web site at: www.josseybass.com

PROMOTION CODE = ND3

CC113   Systems for Offering Concurrent Enrollment at High Schools and
        Community Colleges
        Piedad F. Robertson, Brian G. Chapman, Fred Gaskin
        Offers approaches to creating valuable programs, detailing all the
        components necessary for the success and credibility of concurrent
        enrollment. Focuses on the faculty liaisons from appropriate disciplines that
        provide the framework for an ever-improving program.
        ISBN: 0-7879-5758-5

CC112   Beyond Access: Methods and Models for Increasing Retention and
        Learning Among Minority Students
        Steven R.. Aragon
        Presents practical models, alternative approaches, and new strategies for
        creating effective cross-cultural courses that foster higher retention and
        learning success for minority students. Argues that educational programs
        must now develop a broader curriculum that includes multicultural and
        multi-linguistic information.
        ISBN: 0-7879-5429-2

CC111   How Community Colleges Can Create Productive Collaborations with
        Local Schools
        James C. Palmer
        Details ways that community colleges and high schools can work together to
        help students navigate the difficult passage from secondary to higher educa-
        tion. Provides detailed case studies of actual collaborations between specific
        community colleges and high school districts, discusses legal problems that
        can arise when high school students enroll in community colleges, and more.
        ISBN: 0-7879-5428-4

CC110   Building Successful Relationships Between Community Colleges and the
        Media
        Clifton Truman Daniel, Hanel Henriksen Hastings
        Explores current relationships between two-year colleges and the media
        across the country, reviewing the history of community colleges'
        relationships with members of the press, examining the media's relationships
        with community college practitioners, and offering practical strategies for
        advancing an institution's visibility.
        ISBN: 0-7879-5427-6

CC109   Dimensions of Managing Academic Affairs in the Community College
        Douglas Robillard, Jr.
        Offers advice on fulfilling the CAO's academic duties, and explores the
        CAO's faculty and administrative roles, discussing how to balance the
        sometimes conflicting roles of faculty mentor, advocate, and disciplinarian
        and the importance of establishing a synergistic working relationship with
        the president.
        ISBN: 0-7879-5369-5

CC108   Trends in Community College Curriculum
        Gwyer Schuyler
        Presents a detailed picture of the national community college curriculum,
        using survey data collected in 1998 by the Center for the Study of
        Community Colleges. Chapters analyze approaches to general education,
        vocational course offerings, the liberal arts, multicultural education, ESL,
        honors programs, and distance learning.
        ISBN: 0-7879-4849-7

CC107   **Gateways to Democracy: Six Urban Community College Systems**
        Raymond C. Bowen, Gilbert H. Muller
        Features case studies of six prototypical urban community college systems,
        exploring how they meet the educational and training needs of an
        increasingly diverse ethnic and racial community.
        ISBN: 0-7879-4848-9

CC106   **Understanding the Impact of Reverse Transfer Students on Community
        Colleges**
        Barbara K. Townsend
        Examines institutions' strategies for recruiting, retaining, and serving reverse
        transfer students and reveals how the presence of reverse transfer students
        affects policy-making.
        ISBN: 0-7879-4847-0

CC105   **Preparing Department Chairs for Their Leadership Roles**
        Rosemary Gillett-Karam
        Presents the qualities that experienced department chairs cite as being
        crucial to success and makes a persuasive argument for the need to develop
        formal training programs for people newly appointed to these positions.
        ISBN: 0-7879-4846-2

CC104   **Determining the Economic Benefits of Attending Community College**
        Jorge R. Sanchez, Frankie Santos Laanan
        Discusses various state initiatives that look at student outcomes and
        institutional accountability efforts and analyzes the trend to connect
        accountability and outcome measures with funding.
        ISBN: 0-7879-4237-5

CC103   **Creating and Benefiting from Institutional Collaboration: Models for
        Success**
        Dennis McGrath
        Examines the many ways collaboration both benefits and alters the
        participating organizations, offering practical examples and lessons learned
        that can be used by a variety of institutions in their efforts to foster
        collaborative relationships.
        ISBN: 0-7879-4236-7

CC102   **Organizational Change in the Community College: A Ripple or a Sea
        Change?**
        John Stewart Levin
        Presents real-life examples of community colleges' experiences with
        organizational change—both successful and unsuccessful—and examines
        organizational change through a variety of theoretical frameworks, including
        feminism and postmodernism.
        ISBN: 0-7879-4235-9

CC101   **Integrating Technology on Campus: Human Sensibilities and Technical
        Possibilities**
        Kamala Anandam
        Addresses the topics of organizational structures, comprehensive economic
        planning, innovative policies and procedures, faculty development, and
        above all, collaborative approaches to achieving significant and enduring
        results from technological applications.
        ISBN: 0-7879-4234-0

CC100   Implementing Effective Policies for Remedial and Developmental
        Education
        Jan M. Ignash
        Addresses specific policy questions involved in the debate over remedial and
        developmental education and uses national and state data, as well as
        information from case studies of individual institutions, to provide insights
        into effective approaches to remedial and developmental education.
        ISBN: 0-7879-9843-5

CC99   Building a Working Policy for Distance Education
        Connie L. Dillon, Rosa Cintron
        Presents some of the policy issues confronting higher education in the age of
        distance learning, and discusses the implications of these issues for the
        community college.
        ISBN: 0-7879-9842-7

CC98   Presidents and Trustees in Partnership: New Roles and Leadership
        Challenges
        Iris M. Weisman, George B. Vaughan
        Explores the professional needs, challenges, and roles of community college
        governing board members and their presidents—and how these factors
        influence the board-president team.
        ISBN: 0-7879-9818-4

CC97   School-to-Work Systems: The Role of Community Colleges in Preparing
        Students and Facilitating Transitions
        Edgar I. Farmer, Cassy B. Key
        Demonstrates how community colleges are engaged in strengthening
        existing partnerships with schools, employers, and labor- and community-
        based organizations as they develop new programs to address the three
        major components of school-to-work systems.
        ISBN: 0-7879-9817-6

CC96   Transfer and Articulation: Improving Policies to Meet New Needs
        Tronie Rifkin
        Presents recommendations for current and future transfer and articulation
        policies in an attempt to expand the discourse and thereby enhance the
        ability of community colleges to serve their own educational goals as well as
        the educational goals of this nation.
        ISBN: 0-7879-9893-1

CC95   Graduate and Continuing Education for Community College Leaders:
        What It Means Today
        James C. Palmer, Stephen G. Katsinas
        Provides critical perspectives on the current status of community college
        education as an academic specialty.
        ISBN: 0-7879-9892-3

CC89   Gender and Power in the Community College
        Barbara K. Townsend
        Examines the gender socialization that results in stereotypes that usually
        operate to women's disadvantage socially, politically, and economically and
        explores ways the community college experience can be structured to
        overcome this disadvantage.
        ISBN: 0-7879-9913-X